UNHOOKED

&
untangled

A GUIDE TO FINDING *freedom* FROM
YOUR VICES, ADDICTIONS, AND BAD HABITS

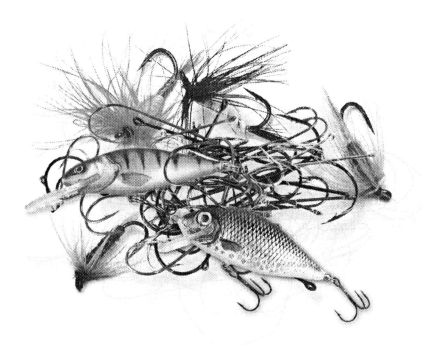

Unhooked & Untangled

A guide to finding freedom from your
vices, addictions, and bad habits

Eric Dykstra | Bruce Rauma

CROSSING CHURCH
PUBLISHING
freegrace.tv
Guilt free. Grace full.

We dedicate this book to every person who is
desperate to make it through the next 24 hours.

We know you feel lost, broken
and weak, but you are not alone.

God is with you.
You will find freedom.

May this book help guide you on your
journey and take you to the destiny you long for.

Thanks from Eric

First, I want to thank Jesus Christ for freeing me from approval addiction and workaholism. Thank you for giving me a new lease on life. That month you met me in Florida changed me forever, brought me more happiness than I've ever had, and taught me about grace.

Secondly, to my Kelly. You set aside tons of time and energy to help make this project a reality. More than that, you have walked with me through every hard day I've ever experienced. You kept me sane. Your voice and encouragement helped get me out of bed and guide me to a better life. Your refusal to give up when things were really hard gave me the strength I needed to keep moving forward and be happy and healthy again. I love you like spring rain.

Third, I want to thank Tracy Keech. Your red pen is magical. Your long hours of reading and gracefully suggesting adjustments to my words made this project a huge success. Thanxs fer currecting me so I dont rite like a ignerant pursan.

Lastly, to Bruce Rauma. You and I have fought side-by-side through some hellish battles against the evil one. We have seen each other on our worst days and still call each other friend. Thanks for sitting with me at that steakhouse in South Carolina where I cried and wept and wanted to quit. Thanks for letting me get all up in your grill outside your house that day when we smoked cigars and I wouldn't let you quit. I wrote this book with you, not only because you are the smartest person I know when it comes to recovery, but also because you know how to take some pretty serious hits and keep standing. I love you, bro.

Thanks from Bruce

I want to thank Jesus Christ for saving a wretch like me. You loved me enough to meet me in a place where I totally blew you off and still offered me Your amazing grace. You are my Leader and my Lord, and I will always keep You first in my life.

I want to thank my wife, Diane. You are a strong woman and are tenacious about helping broken people. You encourage and inspire me to be a better person. I love you more than you know. You are my best friend, and I can't imagine life without you.

I need to thank Jeff and Dena Bergman, who selflessly served alongside us for so many years to share the hope and healing of Jesus.

Thank you to all of the Crossing Recovery leaders who have led with us. You have given so much of your hearts and lives to end addiction in Minnesota. I am grateful for you all.

Minnesota Adult and Teen Challenge and Lindner Media Productions, thank you for your hospitality and the opportunities.

Tracy Keech, you have been my longtime friend and put so many hours into the construction of this book. You are amazing at what you do and an exemplary leader. Your wisdom and passion for Jesus and recovery is contagious. Plus, your husband is really cool. Thank you for your hard work and dedication to see this project through.

Pastors Eric and Kelly, you are my spiritual parents. You have helped me in more ways than I could ever count. You push me to success, tolerate my shortcomings, and love me through it all. You are the best leaders, amazing pastors, and really great friends. You bravely and radically move hundreds of lives to Jesus and His grace, and for that I am so grateful. Thank you for allowing me to serve under your leadership and live out my calling with you.

What people are saying about Unhooked & Untangled

Both of us are die-hard fishermen, born-again Christians, and have a heart for addicts. *Unhooked & Untangled* combines fishing, faith, and freedom found in recovery. Pastors Eric and Bruce have put our three favorite passions together, and we love this book!

- Al and Ron Lindner Founders of *In-Fisherman*,
Angling Edge, lindnermedia.com

Since Christ "unhooked" me, I actually enjoy my life--raising my kid, jamming with KoRn, anything I do. It's the best high ever. I hope you read this book, get free, and move on to the life you really want to live.

- Brian "Head" Welch KoRn, Love & Death, New York Times best-selling author of *Save Me From Myself* and *Stronger*

Unhooked & Untangled starts and ends with grace for you-- however you got where you are, and wherever you go from here. In the middle, you'll find a faith-based approach to freedom from what lures you. This book has hope for anyone who just wants to be set free to thrive.

- Jud Wilhite author of *The God of Yes*,
Senior Pastor of Central Christian Church

Pastors Eric and Bruce use wisdom, boldness, and compassion to articulate a healthy path toward obtaining the true desire of all humanity: Freedom. If you are sick and tired of dog-paddling your way through vices, additions, and bad habits, then reading *Unhooked & Untangled* is a must for you.

- Anthony Bass MN Adult & Teen Challenge, former NFL player

My prayer is that this book will unhook many, many people-- like my brother--who is homeless, due to his addictions. As I have experienced my own addicted past, I believe God's word that, "Greater is He that is in you, than He that is in the world." Thank you Eric and Bruce, for putting your own battles and victories into this book. It is going to reach many fish, and set them free.

- Heather Palacios Blogger/Writer/Speaker | wondherful.com

TABLE OF CONTENTS

PREFACE

This is a foundational book to get you started in a lifestyle of recovery.

We believe that you can be totally set free by the grace of God.

We know that your vice, addiction, or bad habit might have you hooked right now, but we also know that God is bigger than any addiction, and He will set you free as your begin to walk in relationship with Him.

Our core beliefs are driven by the Bible, so we will be referencing scripture a lot.

Our hope and prayer is that you would see the value of what Jesus teaches in scripture so you can learn to live a

happy,

healthy,

and **free life**.

INTRODUCTION - OUR ADMISSION

**Read this so you know who we are
and what we're all about.**

Everyone says the first step toward recovery is admission, so before you read this book, we need to admit some things to you.

This will help you know who we are,
where we are coming from,
and what our goals are for you.

Here goes:

We are addicts.

We admit it.

Bruce spent 14 years as an alcoholic and Eric spent many years as a workaholic and approval addict. These behaviors destroyed our lives, ruined our relationships, and kept us from our potential.

We understand how vices, addictions, and bad habits can hook us and **pull us away from our destiny**.

Expect to hear our personal struggles, pain, and heartbreak along the way.

We know what it's like to be hooked.

We are fishermen.

We admit it.

We love to fish.

Bruce loves to musky fish, and Eric loves to fish for smallmouth bass. We spend our summers seeking to hook big fish, getting up early and staying out late on the water.

When we set out to write a book about addiction and recovery, it was only natural that we'd write in fishing terms.

Our world is viewed through the lenses of fishing, so expect to see much of this subject explained through the eyes of two men that spend their lives hooking and unhooking fish.

We are Jesus-followers.

We admit it.

We believe that Jesus and His grace are the ONLY way people can truly experience freedom.

Bruce encountered Christ on a set of railroad tracks, surrendering his life after hitting rock bottom.

Eric has had two encounters with Christ.

Once at age seventeen, when he first gave his life to Jesus, and again at age thirty-eight, when He finally comprehended the grace of God.

Expect to hear how our encounters with Jesus and His grace changed our thinking and behaviors, and **set us free** from the vices that had hooked us for so long.

We are pastors.

We admit it.

Bruce has been a pastor for seven years, and Eric for fifteen.

You might be tempted to think that this must make us super-spiritual. You might think that we have it all together.

This could not be further from the truth!

Pastors aren't perfect.

We're real people who still fight temptation.

We battle vices,
addictions,
and bad habits
every day.

However, now that we have encountered Christ, we have a power we did not possess before.

We have the supernatural power of Jesus and His grace.

Expect to hear how the power of Jesus has helped us in our roles as leaders in the church world.

We love life.

We admit it.

We believe God has a great destiny for us.

Now that Jesus has cut the line to our addictions and vices, we get to live the life we always dreamed of!

We believe this for you, too.

We believe once you're unhooked, you can swim off to your destiny!

Our goal is that you will enjoy living again.

We want you to pursue your dreams.

We want you to be who God created you to be!

We want you to experience what Jesus promised: "*...life to the full." (John 10:10)*

So let's get started.

You are about to get UNHOOKED!

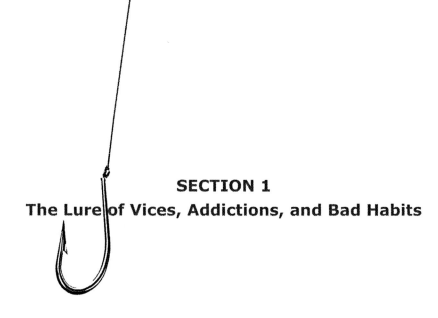

SECTION 1
The Lure of Vices, Addictions, and Bad Habits

Chapter 1
Immersed in a World of Temptation

"Lead me not into temptation.
I can find the way myself."
- Jane Seabrook

We love to fish!

We'll spend hundreds of hours in the summer on the water trying to catch smallmouth bass, musky, and the occasional northern pike.

Fish are immersed in a very different world than us. They're surrounded by water. They spend their lives immersed in it, looking for food.

Fish are just trying to survive in their hostile environment.

Their daily struggle is "eat or be eaten."

Lures,
hooks,
and temptations
are dangled in their faces,
trying to pull them away from the **life they want to live.**

This same thing is true for us.

You and I are immersed in a sinful, fallen, temptation-filled world.

We are trying to survive in a hostile environment filled with hooks, lures, and shiny things.

In a moment, these things can **sink their barbs in** and pull us away from God's divine destiny for us.

The Bible talks about this hostile, temptation-filled world that we live in.

1 John 2:16 *For the world offers only a craving for physical pleasure, a craving for everything we see, and pride in our achievements and possessions. These are not from the Father, but are from this world. (NLT)*

Think about your environment for a minute.

What are the cravings that tend to hook you, hurt you, and pull you away from the life God designed you to live?

Here's a big list to get you thinking (circle all that apply to you):

Illegal drugs
Alcohol
Prescription drugs
Cutting
Sexual misconduct
Porn
Overeating
Anger
Smoking
Swearing
Gambling
Money
Shopping
Fantasy
Overworking
Approval of others
Other _____

> **Stop beating yourself up over your cravings!**
>
> **You are immersed in a world of temptation!**

We want you to know something really important about the thing(s) you just circled.

Stop beating yourself up over your cravings!

You are immersed in a world of temptation!

The reason you are hooked and in the situation you are in is partially because you live in a world that is FILLED with temptation.

Your environment is hostile to you.

It is actually quite a miracle you are doing as well as you are!

We bring this up because many people believe they must be really messed up to have the struggles they face.

They believe they are worse than other people, and that they are not normal - but this is not the case!

You are totally normal, you just live in a world that is hostile to you.

It has hooked you
and hurt you
and trained you
to crave
and think
and act
the way you do!

Let us give you a few examples from our lives.

Eric grew up in a very conservative, authoritarian church world that was driven by approval.

As long as he did the right thing, never messed up, followed all the rules, and always achieved, approval was given.

Teachers, pastors, and church leaders would give all kinds of accolades to those who produced their version of good behavior. However, the second you slacked off, "backslid," or sinned in any way, you were attacked.

People looked down on you, talked bad about you behind your back, and made you feel condemned and embarrassed.

Because of this environment, Eric developed all sorts of coping mechanisms. He developed all kinds of **destructive cravings** and behaviors and attitudes to survive in his pressure-filled church.

He worked crazy hours (70-80 hours in a week) just so people would approve of him.

He was afraid of disappointing people.

He would go into a massive depression if he got criticized.

He would freak out at the smallest mistake, because he feared failure and condemnation from others.

He sacrificed relationships on the altar of accomplishment.

He put on a front of spirituality so people would respect him and say nice things about him.

These coping mechanisms were learned in order to navigate his hostile environment.

He was **programmed** to be like this.

Bruce's environment was totally different, but was just as hostile and destructive.

He grew up with a wonderful family, but insecurity and approval-seeking were deeply rooted in his life.

He felt he needed the approval of every type of person, including the drug dealers and the partiers.

At the early age of fourteen, Bruce decided to win this group's approval.

The more he hung around this
dysfunctional crowd of people,
the more his
life started to unravel.

Fifteen years later,
he found himself
alone,
drunk,
and addicted.

The only people who would tolerate his behavior were a few
fellow addicts and drunks.

He was hurt,
scared,
angry,
tired of life,
and **frustrated with God**.

We tell you these stories because we want you to understand
that your addictions, vices, and bad habits come partially from
your environment.

You must recognize that you have been immersed in a hostile
world, and this is why you have become the person you never
wanted to be.

It is not that you are
worse than others,
or abnormal from most,
you have just been
living in a world
that's out to
destroy you.

You've learned terrible habits as a way to cope with a terrible
world.

Now that you know that, here's some good news.

1 John 4:4 *...greater is He that is IN you, than he that is IN
the world. (KJV)*

The fact that the world you are immersed in is hostile doesn't
mean you are going to lose the battle of addiction!

If you invite **CHRIST** into your life, **HE IS GREATER** than your hostile environment!

And if HE lives in you, the GREATER ONE will help you conquer what you could never conquer alone!

Jesus IS GREATER
than your background,
your programming,
your cravings,
and your struggles!

Jesus IS GREATER
than your hurts
and family upbringing.

Jesus IS GREATER
than a bad home life
and hurtful parents.

Jesus is greater.

If you invite Him into your life, you will see the GREATER ONE conquer the destructive coping mechanisms that you learned being immersed in this fallen world.

Right now you can either see your vice, addiction, or bad habit as greater, or you can see Jesus as greater.

Whatever you believe will determine your ability to conquer what has hooked you for so long!

We want to end this chapter by telling you two things:

1. Many of you have been immersed in your temptation-filled, toxic environment for so long, you need to get out of it in order to get to free. We recommend that you go to an in-patient treatment program for a minimum of 30 days.

2. We encourage you to focus on the unhooked life that Jesus died to give you. Start by writing out a Faith Statement that can help you focus on the Greater One. We will write our faith statements and give you room to write down yours as well.

We believe Jesus is GREATER than our addiction, vice or bad habit of _____.

YOU: _____

_____

_____

_____

_____

We believe Jesus IN us is GREATER than _____ that is hurting us or holding us back.

YOU: _____

_____

_____

_____

_____

We invite Jesus Christ and His GREATER POWER into our lives today. We ask for His GREATER POWER to conquer _____ today in us.

YOU: _____

_____

_____

_____

Now write out those statements on a notecard and put them on your bathroom mirror or a prominent place where you will see it every day.

Repeat them out loud daily, until you truly believe it.

> **Your environment may have helped make you,**
>
> **BUT Jesus is beginning to remake you, because HE IS GREATER!**

Chapter 2
Biting the Lure of Addiction

**"Hard to say what's right when
all I wanna do is wrong."**

- Prince

Let's talk about a northern pike for a second.

For those of you that don't live in Minnesota, the northern pike is the wolf of the water world in Minnesota.

It is one of the biggest predators.

It is designed to attack and eat almost anything smaller than itself that moves in the water.

It will eat other fish, frogs, small ducks...
Basically, if it moves and can fit in its mouth, it is gone.

One time Eric hooked a 10-inch largemouth bass and was reeling it in. A northern saw the movement of the bass and viciously attacked it.

By the time he got the bass to the boat, it was dead as a doornail and all torn to pieces.

The northern couldn't help himself.

It's his nature to instinctively follow and bite whatever looks like food to him.

Muskies are the same way.

One time Bruce hooked a 5-pound northern, and a giant musky grabbed it, simply because it instinctively had to.

Fish are pre-programmed to attack movement in the water.

The same is true for human beings.

One of the main reasons it is so hard to say "NO" to our addictions, vices, and bad habits is because we have an instinctive nature that is pre-programmed to sin.

We can't help it.

When we see a vice, addiction, or bad habit presented in a certain way, we instinctively bite.

> **When we see a vice, addiction, or bad habit presented in a certain way, we instinctively bite.**

When a hot girl offers herself, men agree.

When a friend offers a joint, we say yes.

When we get some extra money, gambling with it seems like a great idea.

We're pre-programmed to **do the wrong thing**.

We know some of you might be skeptical of this, so let us explain.

The Bible says mankind started out perfect, but then our original parents, Adam and Eve, sinned and ate the forbidden fruit.

This cursed mankind forever. (See Genesis 3)

Every descendant of Adam and Eve (you and I) has been pre-programmed (or cursed) because of sin.

Now we have something in us that naturally wants to do the wrong thing.

Here is how you can know that is true. Do you have to teach a child to do the right thing or the wrong thing?

This is obvious.

Children must be taught to do the right thing, because they naturally do the wrong thing.

No parent has
ever had to
teach a child
to lie,
be selfish,
or disobey.

We come by all these characteristics naturally.

We are pre-programmed to sin.

Here are a few Bible verses so you get the concept:

Psalm 51:5 *For I was born a sinner—yes, from the moment my mother conceived me. (NLT)*

We were all **born sinners**.

It is our nature to gravitate to addictions, vices, and bad habits like a fish is pre-programmed to bite a lure.

Romans 3:10-12 *No one is righteous—not even one. No one is truly wise; no one is seeking God. All have turned away; all have become useless. No one does good, not a single one. (NLT)*

This scripture teaches us that **no one is perfect**.

No one is capable of not sinning and doing the right thing all the time. This is why, when you tell yourself, "I am going to quit! It is going to be different this time!" it never works.

Your own **willpower** alone is **incapable of changing you**.

Here is the most crystal-clear Bible verse about the topic of our natural inclination to sin:

James 1:14-15 *Temptation comes from our own desires, which entice us and drag us away. These desires give birth to sinful actions. And when sin is allowed to grow, it gives birth to death. (NLT)*

This scripture reveals to us the pattern of our addiction.

Our inner desire and nature leads us to the lure of sin.

When we see it or think about it, we instinctively want it.

We grab the bait, unable to turn away.

The devil then sets the hook and his barb goes deep into our souls.

He begins to reel us in.

No matter how hard we struggle, **we end up dead**.

[For Eric, this is so true. If he were to go back to a life of workaholism, every relationship that's important to him would die. If Bruce were to have one more drink, it could lead to his literal death.]

This is true for all of us.

Addictions,
vices,
or bad habits
slowly **kill**
you and
everything you love.

You want to get away, but it just seems like you can't.

We are incapable of changing ourselves.

We are hardwired to sin.

We know what you're thinking... *"That is terrible! Is our willpower really that incapable of changing us?"*

YES!
Willpower alone is never enough.

You can't throw off addiction in your own strength long-term! You might make it a few days or weeks, but in the end it hooks you back in and you are back where you started.

Jeremiah 13:23 *Can an Ethiopian change his skin or a leopard its spots? Neither can you do good who are accustomed to doing evil.*

See, once we have become accustomed to bad behavior (and we all are), we become incapable of change.

Just like we can't change the color of our skin, and a leopard can't get rid of its spots, our own willpower is never enough.

So how do we get free?

If we can never change ourselves, how do we conquer what hooks us?

The answer is pretty simple:

We must **exchange our willpower** for **His mighty power!**

Jesus Christ knows we can't escape our struggles, so He promised to give us supernatural power to conquer what hooks us.

(That is what Mile Marker 3 is all about. For now, we will just summarize this concept, but we will thoroughly unpack it in Chapter 9.)

This is how the Apostle Paul writes it:

***Ephesians 1:19-20** I also pray that you will understand the incredible greatness of God's power **FOR US** who believe him. This is the **<u>SAME MIGHTY POWER</u>** that raised Christ from the dead... (NLT)*

Whoa! Did you see that?

The same mighty power that raised Christ from the dead is available for us who believe right now!

Think about that.

That is the **greatest power in the universe!**

No one can resurrect the dead, and no one can resurrect him/herself. Yet, JESUS DID THIS!

He has the power to resurrect the dead, and He offers this power to you for what you need conquered in your life!

Jesus says,
"Come to me.
Follow me.
Trust in me!

Stop trying to
fix yourself with
your own willpower,
and trust
MY MIGHTY POWER!"

What if you exchanged your willpower for His mighty power today? What if this became your prayer?

Jesus, I recognize I cannot, with my own willpower, change my life. I am incapable of conquering my addiction, vice, or bad habit.

BUT I KNOW YOU CAN CONQUER THIS FOR ME!

Today I rest in your mighty power.

26

Today I trust that You will give me the ability, strength, and power to say NO to my sinful nature and yes to freedom!

I trust You alone for my freedom.

Why not take a few minutes and write out a prayer like that to Jesus?

Include the following:

- Acknowledge your willpower is not strong enough to conquer your addiction, vice, or bad habit.

- Ask Him to exchange your willpower for His mighty power.

- Commit to trusting His power alone to change your life.

- Commit to live today letting His power conquer your vice, addiction, or bad habit, and let Him guide your life.

Chapter 3
Our Enemy is Always Casting

"The devil pulls the strings that make us dance..."
- Charles Baudelaire

You have to determine what kind of fish you want to catch before you ever go fishing.

You choose your target,
determine what bait or lures
that species is likely to bite,
and then you gear up for the attack.

When Eric goes fishing, he is usually after smallmouth bass on the river near his home. He mostly fishes with orange, yellow, or bronze-colored spinner baits because he knows that is what a smallie in the river is most likely to strike.

When Bruce goes out on the water, he is usually only after muskies.

Muskies are the largest predatory fish in Minnesota. They are consistently caught in the 45-50 inch range.

So, Bruce fishes with lures that are 12-16 inches in length. He fishes with lures that are as big as the bass that Eric is casting for.

It takes this size lure to attract a musky.

To catch a fish like a musky, you must cast lures that a musky will attack.

The same is true for the devil.

The devil is smart.

He is always
trolling around
for a victim,
and he knows
just what lures
to throw at us
to hook our life
and **destroy** our soul.

The Apostle Peter said it like this:

1 Peter 5:8 *Stay alert! Watch out for your great enemy, the devil. He prowls around like a roaring lion, looking for someone to devour. (NLT)*

The devil is always on the prowl.

He and his minions are searching the whole earth to catch victims.

He does not quit.

He is patient.

He lies in wait.

He looks for just the
right opportunity,
and then he strikes.

He dangles
the right bait
at the right time
in front of you,
and **you get hooked**.

Let us give you an example.

Here's how Bruce was hooked:

> **The devil is
> always on
> the prowl.**
>
> **He does
> not quit.**
>
> **He is patient.**
>
> **He lies in
> wait.**
>
> **He looks for
> just the right
> opportunity,
> and then he
> strikes.**

32

It was a subtle presentation. Bruce ended up an alcoholic over a long period of time.
There wasn't a day when he woke up and thought, "I think I'll be an alcoholic, that sounds like fun."

No, there was a series of events that had to take place to create the perfect storm in his life.

The **alcoholism**.

First was a lack of relationships.

As we mentioned before, Bruce always wanted to fit in with everyone. He was always desperate to make people like him. He began to believe he would be better liked if he drank and partied.

So, at age fourteen, Bruce got drunk for the first time - and the devil set his hook!

By the time the magic age of twenty-one arrived, he no longer had to sneak around and try to buy liquor underage. He could drive to the bar, have as many drinks as he wanted, and just go home.

It was so easy.

It made sense.

The hooks went in **deeper** still.

This bar-scene lifestyle soon spiraled out of control. It wasn't enough to hit the bar once a week with friends, like a lot of people.

He began to believe he needed to get high and drunk every day, even at work. Here is Bruce's lunch break routine every day for seven long years:

Leave work at noon.

Jump in the truck to drive to the liquor store.

33

Sometimes, not always, smoke marijuana on the way to get beer.

Run in and get a six-pack.

Get back in the truck. Start slamming beer.

Finish up the six-pack in the drive thru getting fast food tacos.

Get back on the road and head back to the office.

Halfway back, put the empty cans in the back seat.

Put the pot pipe away.

Finish the tacos.

Smoke a cigarette.

Put Visine in eyes.

Get back to work.

Total time: thirty-three minutes.

Did we mention this was just lunch?

This **cycle of insanity** seemed normal to Bruce every workday, and nobody knew!

The rest of his day was just as crazy.

He'd pick up another twelve-pack and a bottle of gin at the liquor store on the way home from work. At the time, liquor stores closed at eight o'clock. Ten minutes before eight o'clock every night, he'd realize that he didn't buy enough. So, back in the truck and down to the liquor store he'd go again.

Other times, he'd scramble to get to the bar to finish out the evening. At bar close or around one o'clock in the morning, he'd hurry home to bed only to wake up at five and do it all over again.
Weekend party nights became just another night.

Pretty soon, every night was party night.

Weekend party friends would call early in the week to make plans for Friday or Saturday night, but Bruce wanted Tuesday night to be great, too. You know, because it was always ladies night at some bar or another.

Specific friendships were formed with other alcoholics who could go out with him mid-week to get him to the weekend, when all of the "real" friends were ready to go party.

The hook was in deep.

Satan kept saying things like this to Bruce, "Why bother getting free? You can't change, and it wouldn't really be better to be sober anyway. No one cares about you."

As Bruce believed
these lies,
he really believed
his life
was useless,
purposeless,
meaningless,
and hopeless.

Then came rock bottom.

After living this way for fifteen years, Bruce found himself on the kitchen floor in his townhome one night. He and his roommate had gotten drunk.

In a moment of clarity,
Bruce said, **"I don't want to do this anymore."**

Little did he know that this was his first admission statement.

His roommate wasn't interested in quitting, but he agreed that Bruce had a serious problem, and maybe treatment was his answer.

He said, "I dare you to get up tomorrow and look yourself in the mirror and make a commitment not to drink. Then instead of doing what you normally do everyday, go to an out-patient treatment meeting tomorrow night.

Listen to what they have to say. If it doesn't work, well we'll get drunk then."

This was the statement that started to loosen the hook of Bruce's addiction.

Eric, too, knows the pain of being pulled in by Satan's lies and temptation.

Fear of being ignored was the **bait Satan used** for him.

Eric grew up as the weird kid.

He never really fit in at school, and he only had a few friends.

He always felt left out by the popular kids, so when he went off to college, he vowed things were going to be different.

He was going to succeed and impress everyone around him.

He got great grades.

He started campus initiatives to help inner-city kids.

He served as an unpaid intern at a mega-church.

He launched evangelism efforts to reach people far from God.

He worked at being impressive and popular.

All of that sounds really noble, except he was doing these things partially as a reaction to his childhood hurts.

He was responding to the deep rejection he experienced in childhood and was now trying to impress others so he would never feel that pain again.

Internally, he HAD TO be part of the in-crowd and be popular among the church people he knew.

He was afraid
of being
left out,
overlooked,
and ignored.

It worked.
He increased in popularity.
People were impressed with him.
They learned his name and knew his accomplishments.

But what was secretly going on was **approval addiction**.

He had to be impressive at all costs.

He had to make a name for himself.

He had to get noticed and recognized for his achievements.

All of this stemmed from his fear of being ignored or overlooked.

This fear eventually drove him to **workaholism**.

Eric would work up to 17-18 hours in a day.

He drank 2-3 pots of coffee per day and slept only a few hours a night at one ministry job.

He developed severe migraines from all the lack of sleep and over-caffeination.

One day, after moving to Minnesota and starting this crazy work cycle all over again at another job, his wife, Kelly, couldn't take it anymore.

She looked at him and said, "Eric you are losing me. If you don't change, I won't leave you, but this marriage is going to die."

That was the statement that started to break Satan's power in Eric's life.

This was his rock bottom.

He looked at his life and it finally hit him - he was sacrificing everything on the altar of approval of others, success, and accomplishment.

All of this started because Satan whispered in his ear, "No one likes you. You are never going to amount to anything. You are always going to be on the outside looking in. You will always be overlooked and ignored."

See, Satan knows just what bait to use to hook and destroy us.

His strategy is always the same, and it is two-fold. Let's take a minute and talk about the two-fold fishing strategy of the devil.

1. Satan waits until we are at our weakest.

The devil is a roaring lion... (1 Peter 5:8)

Think about a lion for a second.

Does it attack when its prey is at full strength? No!

He waits
until
his prey
is alone,
or weak,
or sick, and then...

he attacks.

This is what the devil does with us!

He waits until we are alone, then he attacks. Or he waits until we are at our weak point, or feeling down and discouraged.

This is when we must be on our guard!

Maybe you have heard this before, but it bears repeating.

Whenever you are:

Hungry

Angry

Lonely or

Tired - HALT!

Don't ever go near anything that might trigger your addiction, vice, or bad habit when you are at your weak point! Just stay away when you are feeling weak!

The Apostle Paul says it like this:

2 Timothy 2:22 *"Flee the evil desires of youth..."*

In other words, RUN, FORREST, RUN! from anything that triggers your desire to indulge!

- If you are struggling with porn, don't use a computer when you are hungry, angry, lonely, or tired.

- If you are struggling with alcohol, don't drive by a bar or liquor store when you are feeling this way.

- If you are struggling with gambling, don't go near the casino or go online when you are in this frame of mind.

Satan attacks when you are at your weakest point.

Run from temptation when you are weak!

A simple way to run from temptation is to call your sponsor, friend, or mentor, and tell them you are struggling. Call them before you give in to the temptation. Ask them to pick you up or meet you for coffee.

Don't try to fight the temptation alone.

You need to get strength from someone who cares about you in order to get you through your weak point.

2. Satan speaks lies to our minds.

Jesus calls the devil the "father of lies" and says that lying is his "native language" (John 8:44). Satan can't make us give in to our temptations, so he must lie to us and get us to believe these lies are truth. Then we become willing to choose to do the wrong thing so he can destroy us.

This is what he did to our first parents.

He lied to Eve in the Garden of Eden.

Just look at the way he messed with Eve's mind and lied to her in Genesis 3:

Genesis 3:3-5 [Eve said], "It's only the fruit from the tree in the middle of the garden that we are not allowed to eat. God said, 'You must not eat it or even touch it; if you do, you will die.'" "You won't die!" the serpent replied to the woman. "God knows that your eyes will be opened as soon as you eat it, and you will be like God, knowing both good and evil."

The devil blatantly told Eve the *opposite* of what God said.

She believed him,
ate the forbidden fruit,
and destroyed her life.

This is how Satan works in all our lives.

He told Eric, "You're overlooked. You need to prove yourself."

Eric believed that lie and became a workaholic, approval-addict.

He told Bruce, "You must do whatever it takes to fit in."

Bruce believed that lie, and Bruce became an alcoholic.

Satan lies.

When we take the bait and believe the lie, we destroy our own lives.

We do the work for him!

Now let us give you some good news!

If you could become aware of the lies Satan is telling you, recognize them, and ignore them, you could overcome temptation and defeat the devil!

Think of it like fishing again.

Once a fish recognizes that the lure in front of him is a fake with hooks all over it, he will avoid it and live a long and happy life.

> **Once a fish recognizes that the lure in front of him is a fake with hooks all over it, he will avoid it and live a long and happy life.**

A fish that learns to recognize phony baits stays free!

The same is true for you.

You can learn to recognize the lies Satan is telling you!

You can begin to avoid temptation!

You can learn to spot his hooks, and you can live happy and free!

The Apostle Paul says it like this:

2 Corinthians 10:5 *"...take captive every thought and make it obedient to Christ."*

With every thought that pops into your head, grab it and hold it captive. Analyze that thought and see if it's a lie of the devil or the truth of God.

Put every thought through the fishing net filter of Christ's words.

If it doesn't match up with God's truth in the Bible, catch it and throw it out!

When you begin to do this with every thought, every minute, you will be able to stay free from every lie the devil throws at you.

John 8:32 [Jesus said], "Then you will know the truth, and the truth will set you free."

Take a minute and think:

What lies are you believing that cause you to give in to your addiction, vice, or bad habit? Those lies are the root cause of your vice, addiction, and bad habits.

Take a minute and ask God to reveal Satan's lies to you, then write them down here.

Write as many as you can think of. He uses more than one! The more you can think of, the freer you will become!

Now pray to renounce each lie and replace it with the truth.

For example, this is a prayer Eric prayed to break the lies of approval and feelings of rejection and being overlooked:

In the powerful name of Jesus Christ, I, Eric Dykstra, renounce the lie of being overlooked, rejected, and needing to prove myself.

I break all agreements I made with Satan, his servants, their works and effects, on all levels and in all dimensions, in relationship to needing approval from others and feelings of being ignored.

I believe the truth of Jesus Christ and His Word that I am already approved by God because of Jesus.

I am never overlooked, because I am in front of God's mind at all times. I do not have to work like crazy to get others to like me.

God will never reject me.

I can trust that God is working on my behalf to cause the work of my hands to succeed, and that people will find me interesting and valuable in the world.

I now know the truth, and the truth will set me free of my addiction. In Jesus' name I pray. AMEN!

Praying like this frees us from our temptation and moves us into a place of victory.

Now it's your turn. Fill in the blanks with each lie you wrote down and read these prayers out loud to God:

In the Powerful Name of Jesus Christ, I _____ renounce the lie of _____.

I break all agreements I made with Satan, his servants, their works and effects, on all levels and in all dimensions, in relationship to _____.

I believe the truth of Jesus Christ and His Word that I am: (What is the opposite of the lie? If you don't know, ask God to reveal it to you and write it below.)

_____

_____

_____

I can trust that God is working on my behalf to:

_____

_____

_____

I now know the truth, and the truth will set me free of my addiction. In Jesus' name I pray. AMEN!

Satan can't hook you and defeat you if you can recognize the lies he uses as bait to destroy you.

Pray off every lie you can think of, and you will start to walk free of your addiction, vice, or bad habit.

SECTION 2
Jesus Unhooks the Hooked!

Chapter 4

Jesus is our Savior; not our own Self-Effort

"The day we receive Jesus Christ as our
Savior is one of the greatest days of our lives.
Not only are our sins washed away, but God puts
His Spirit inside of us and gives us new desires."

- Joyce Meyer

Let's talk about fishing again!

Have you ever watched a fish struggle to free itself?

It will
thrash,
jump,
roll,
cut left,
cut right,
charge the boat,
run from the boat,
dig down in the weeds -
it will frantically do whatever it can to shake that hook
from its jaw.

But you know what?

A good fisherman sets the hook so hard and deep, plays the
fish so well, and is so in-control, that it is rare for a fish to
shake free.

The same is true for you and me.

Satan is an expert at hooking you.

Your own self-effort - no matter how hard you struggle, no
matter how hard you fight - will rarely ever set you free. But
like a hooked fish, we try anyway, don't we?

We thrash around in a sea of guilt and make all kinds of promises about how we are never going to do this again, only to be back in the same behavior a few days later.

We try all kinds of self-help and practical steps and try to work up greater and greater willpower, but it never seems to work.

This is our insanity.

Albert Einstein defined insanity this way:

Doing the same thing over and over again, and expecting different results.

Many of us live this same way when we get hooked.

We live in this type of cycle:

Drunk, sorry, never gonna do that again...
Drunk, sorry, never gonna do that again...
Drunk, sorry, never gonna do that again...
Drunk, sorry, never gonna do that again...

You get the idea. We struggle in our own self-effort to free ourselves, but it rarely works.

The Bible agrees. In the Old Testament, Solomon the Wise said it like this:

Proverbs 26:11 *"As a dog returns to its vomit, so fools repeat their folly."*

Dogs will re-eat disgusting things without even thinking about it.

People do the same thing.

We go back and repeat our same mistakes over and over and over again. We just can't help it. [*Side note: We are not dogs or fools or insane, but this is the pattern we follow when we are hooked in addictive behaviors.*]

In the New Testament, the Apostle Paul said it like this:

Romans 7:15 *I don't really understand myself, for I want to do what is right, but I don't do it. Instead, I do what I hate. (NLT)*

He just keeps living in a cycle of insanity, doing the wrong thing! He wants to do what is right, but he just can't do it! Can you relate?

He goes on and says:

Romans 7:18-21 *I want to do what is right, but I can't. I want to do what is good, but I don't. I don't want to do what is wrong, but I do it anyway…*

…I have discovered this principle of life—that when I want to do what is right, I inevitably do what is wrong. (NLT)

Wow! His self-effort was not enough. No amount of struggle or fighting caused him to overcome temptation and do the right thing!

So, what do we do?

Do we just live with our addiction, vice, or bad habit forever? NO! Look what Paul says next:

Romans 7:24-25 *Oh, what a miserable person I am! Who will free me from this life that is dominated by sin and death? Thank God! The answer is in Jesus Christ our Lord. (NLT)*

Jesus Christ has the ability to free us!

He is the answer to your vice, addiction, or bad habit.

Though we have an inability to get unhooked, Jesus Christ has the ability to free us!

He is the answer to your vice, addiction, or bad habit.

51

He can free you!

This is what Jesus says about Himself:

Luke 4:18-19 *"The Spirit of the Lord is upon me, for he has anointed me to bring Good News to the poor. <u>He has sent me to proclaim that captives will be released,</u> that the blind will see, that the oppressed will be set free, <u>and that the time of the Lord's favor has come."</u> (NLT)*

In other words, Jesus came to preach good news to you.

He came to tell you that He can set you free from your captivity.

He can cause your eyes to be opened to your problem, and show you the light of a solution.

He can cause the addiction, vice, or bad habit that is oppressing you to be gone.

Over with.

You can be free.

He came to tell you that God has **FAVOR** for you!

Jesus Christ did not come to embarrass you, point out your sins and flaws, and make you feel miserable and condemned.

He came to free you from the stuff that hooks you!

He came to do what your self-effort could never do!

So, what if right now you stopped trusting your own self-effort and began to trust Him to free you?

How do I do that, you ask?

Right now, write out a prayer of trust.

Throw out your self-effort and give your life over to the care of Jesus and His grace!

Start by being honest and telling Jesus you know you can't free yourself. Then tell Jesus you need Him to free you, forgive you, and help you. Then tell Him you believe He can do what you cannot do for yourself.

Take a minute and write out a prayer like that in your own words:

_____

_____

_____

_____

_____

_____

_____

_____

_____

_____

Now that you have released your own self-effort, and are trusting in God's favor (or grace) for your life, we want you to know some of the wonderful things God promises you.

Five promises God gives to those who trust His grace, not their own self-effort:

1. We can reign in life.

Romans 5:17 *...how much more will those who receive God's abundant provision of grace and of the gift of righteousness reign in life through the one man, Jesus Christ.*

When you trust Jesus Christ and His grace, you will reign in life. You will not be defeated forever.

You will **overcome**!

You now have the supernatural ability to conquer whatever vice, addiction, or bad habit you face, because you have the FAVOR (or GRACE) of God on your life.

Fill in the blank and say this out loud:
I can reign in life because God's favor is on me!
_____ will not defeat me!

2. We can be victorious.

Romans 16:20 *The God of peace will soon crush Satan under your feet. May the grace of our Lord Jesus Christ be with you. (NLT)*

When you trust Jesus Christ and His grace, you'll be just fine if Satan attacks. God will crush Satan for you!

Don't try to fight Satan and temptation alone. Ask Jesus to conquer it for you!

Say this out loud:
Jesus Christ, I invite You, in Your grace, to crush Satan's temptation in my life right now! I believe You are stronger than the evil one, and I will be **victorious** because of Your grace to me!

3. We can experience supernatural peace.

2 Peter 1:2 *May grace [God's favor] and peace [perfect well-being, all necessary good, all spiritual prosperity, and freedom from fears and agitating passions and moral conflicts] be multiplied to you in [the full, personal, precise, and correct] knowledge of God and of Jesus our Lord. (AMP)*

When you trust Jesus Christ and His grace, you will experience God's supernatural peace in abundance!

Did you see how the Amplified Bible defines the word "peace"? This is God's promise for those that trust God's grace and not their own self-effort!

Say this out loud:
I believe God's favor is on me, so I have nothing to fear. I can rest and be at peace! Right now, supernatural peace is flooding my soul. I can be calm, **no matter the storm!**

4. We can do the right thing.

2 Corinthians 9:8-9 *And God is able to make all grace abound to you, so that in all things at all times, having all that you need, you will abound in every good work.*

When you trust Jesus Christ and His grace, you will have everything you need to make right choices and do good works instead of bad ones.

You will be able to do the right thing, because of His grace!

Say this out loud:
I know I can do the right thing because Jesus' grace gives me the **supernatural** ability to do right!

5. We can be strong.

2 Timothy 2:1 *You then, my son, be strong in the grace that is in Christ Jesus.*

When you trust Jesus Christ and His Grace, you will have the STRENGTH to do whatever you need to do in life.

Where God's grace is, strength is!

> **Where God's grace is, strength is!**

Say this out loud:

I AM STRONG. Not in my own strength, but in the supernatural grace of Jesus Christ!

Conclusion: This grace vs. self-effort stuff is a big deal.

When Eric was 38, after having been a pastor for more than a decade, he finally came to realize that his own self-effort was not going to help him.

One night while on a vacation in Florida, he stumbled onto the truth of grace. He confessed to God his self-effort, pride, and attempts to do even good things in his own strength.

He made a vow to God to live life in the power of God's grace alone. When he did this, God totally rocked his world.

His life has never been the same.

What if you stopped the self-effort track you are on?

What if you confessed your sin of doing life in your own strength and made a commitment to Christ to ONLY live by His grace and strength?

Write out a prayer telling God what this chapter on self-effort said to you:

Chapter 5
Jesus Did the Work to Set us Free!

"When you look in the eyes of grace,
when you meet grace, when you embrace grace,
when you see the nail prints in grace's hands
and the fire in his eyes, when you feel his relentless
love for you - it will not motivate you to sin.
It will motivate you to righteousness."

- Judah Smith

When you go bass, northern, or musky fishing, you'd better have strong line.

Eric uses 50-pound Power-pro Super Braid, even though most of time the fish he catches are in the five pound range. Bruce uses 80-100 pound test for muskies.

Why so strong?

Because once a fish gets hooked, it will dive under logs, run through the rocks or bury itself in 20 pounds of vegetation. If you don't have super-strong line, many times you will lose the fish because the line will be cut, frayed, or broken.

The same is true with our addictions, vices, and bad habits.

Jesus knew **we could not free ourselves**, so He came and cut the line to the power of sin over us. He uses the supernatural shears of **grace** to break the power of sin in our lives.

The Apostle Paul said it like this:

Romans 6:14 *For sin shall not have dominion over you, for you are not under law but under grace. (NKJV)*

The word "dominion" means "to rule or dominate". Sin CANNOT dominate those who are Christ-followers.

If you have given your life to Christ and stopped trusting in your own strength, you have been cut free of sin because of Jesus and His grace.
How, you ask?

How does grace cut the line to the power of sin over us?

We don't want to get super-theological and technical with you in a book about recovery, but we do want you to understand the power of the cross and all that Jesus did to cut the line to your sin.

So, lean in to this part because it matters.

Let us tell you for a second about the **power of the cross**.

Scripture says you and I are not good or perfect, but Jesus was. Scripture says Jesus never sinned (2 Corinthians 5:21).

He was totally righteous.

This totally perfect, righteous person
came to earth
and
died for our sins.

A perfect person died for imperfect people.
(Romans 5:8)

Think about that for a second! Jesus, in His perfection, knew all about your imperfection! He totally knows the real you and me.

He sees our every flaw and every dark and hidden place,
and He **LOVES US ANYWAY**!

He doesn't just love who we were supposed to be. He loves us as we really are!

> **He doesn't just love who we were supposed to be.**
>
> **He loves us as we really are!**

62

He sees our unrighteousness, badness, unkindness, terrible advice, unhappiness, lack of help, total hypocrisy and flaws and HE LOVES US STILL!

He is proud of us still!

HE WANTS TO BE GOOD TO US STILL!

Not in spite of our sin, but while we are still sinners. This is the **crazy love of God** and the power of the cross.

This is how the Apostle Paul writes about it:

Romans 5:8 *But God showed his GREAT LOVE for us by sending Christ to die for us while we were STILL SINNERS. (NLT)*

Did you see that?

God loves you greatly. Not when you change, but while you are still actively SINNING! While you were still out there in your vice, addiction, and bad habit, He was actively loving you!

He proved this love by dying in our place and taking OUR punishment for all our wrong!

It gets even better:

Romans 5:9 *And since we have been MADE RIGHT in God's sight by the blood of Christ, he will certainly save us from God's CONDEMNATION. (NLT)*

When Jesus died on the cross for you, He covered your sins with His blood. This made you RIGHT in God's eyes.

His blood washed you clean.

YOU ARE RIGHT (or righteous) in His sight, and you're TOTALLY FREE FROM CONDEMNATION!

> **You are right in His sight, and you're totally free from condemnation!**

That is the power of the cross!

Jesus not only forgave our mistakes, but HE MADE US RIGHT!

We are not guilty,
though we have done so many wrong things.
We are not condemned,
though we deserve to be condemned.

God doesn't point out our flaws, failures, and bad choices.
Instead, HE SEES US AS RIGHT or having done the RIGHT
THING!

So now, because of the cross, no matter what you do or say, or
how you act, in Christ Jesus:

You are righteous... in God's eyes.
You are good... in God's eyes.
You are kind... in God's eyes.
You are no longer flawed... in God's eyes.
You are not guilty... in God's eyes!

Why does all of this matter in recovery?

When we know we are not guilty, the power of sin is broken!
We realize we are not that old person we used to be anymore.

Our past has been erased.

We are new people!

We have a new story,
a new Spirit,
and a new strength
that has been given to us as a gift!

We are not addicts anymore; we are SAINTS! Saints do not
give in to temptation. Saints do not want to go back to old
habits.

SAINTS HAVE THE POWER TO DO RIGHT!

This is the power of the cross.

That is the power that is in you, because of Jesus!

You are brand new.

A brand new you doesn't want to go back to the old way of living. Sin's power was broken at the cross!

This is how the Apostle Paul writes it in Colossians:

Colossians 2:13-15 *You were dead because of your sins and because your sinful nature was not yet cut away. Then God made you alive with Christ, for he forgave all our sins. He canceled the record of the charges against us and took it away by nailing it to the cross. In this way, he disarmed the spiritual rulers and authorities. He shamed them publicly by his victory over them on the cross. (NLT)*

When you read those verses, what does it make you think?

_____

_____

_____

_____

Paul uses words & phrases like "cut away" "forgiven" "cancelled" and "nailed" to describe what happened to your old sinful nature at the cross. How does this make you feel?

_____

_____

_____

_____

Paul says that Satan and his minions were "disarmed" at the cross. What does that mean for you and your vice, addiction, or bad habit?

_____

_____

_____

_____

Take a second and think about Jesus and His grace. Do you believe your sins were paid for by Christ? Are you beating yourself up over your sins when they have already been paid for? Thank Christ for taking your punishment:

_____

_____

_____

_____

What vice, addiction or bad habit do you need to remind yourself was "cut away" "forgiven" "cancelled" and "nailed" to the cross?

_____

That sin has no power over you! What can you do to remind yourself that you are not that guy or that girl anymore?

_____

_____

_____

_____

_____

_____

_____

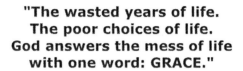

Chapter 6
His River of Grace is Enough

**"The wasted years of life.
The poor choices of life.
God answers the mess of life
with one word: GRACE."**

- Max Lucado

Once grace overwhelms us, we will realize that we don't have to work so hard to find freedom. We can relax and rest in Jesus and His grace, and He will lead us to freedom!

He is our leader,
our strength,
our support,
and our power.

Think about it like a river.

If you were to get in a canoe and launch into a river, you would begin to float downstream. There is a current that naturally pushes you along.

This river supports you,
sends you in a direction,
moves you forward,
guides you,
and it's really hard to fight against.

When you are canoeing downstream, you can sit back, relax, and enjoy the experience, knowing you will make it to your destiny.

God's grace is just like this.

When you give your life to Christ and trust Jesus as your Forgiver and Leader, you enter the river of His grace. He supports you, guides your steps, moves your life forward, empowers you, and eventually you make it to your destiny.

God's never going to stop moving you until you are transformed and make it to the divine destination He planned for you!

That is why we love Jeremiah 29:11 so much.

We suggest you memorize this verse; it will sustain you through your hard days in recovery.

It goes like this:

Jeremiah 29:11 *"For I know the plans I have for you," declares the LORD, "plans to prosper you and not to harm you, plans to give you hope and a future."*

Notice, God has planned your life to make sure you eventually make it!

He has a future for you.

You are going to conquer this vice, addiction, or bad habit that has hooked you!

You just need to stay in the flow of God's grace.

David writes it like this in Psalms:

Psalm 73:24 *You guide me with your counsel, leading me to a glorious destiny. (NLT)*

When you stay in God's river (or flow) of grace and let Him guide you, the only place you can go is a GLORIOUS DESTINY! That is where you are headed: someplace awesome!

Just stay with your guide and go in God's flow of GRACE!

In the New Testament, the Apostle Paul writes it like this:

Philippians 1:6 *...he who began a good work in you will carry it to completion...*

In other words, if God started a work in you and saved you, He will take you all the way to freedom, or completion! He is never going to leave you unfinished.

Rest as He carries you on His river of grace until you arrive at the destination of freedom in Christ.

Here's another thing about rivers: they flow past landmarks.

For example, Eric knows he's almost home when his boat comes around the river bend and he can see the big tree and rope swing that marks his property.

On God's river of grace, there are landmarks as well.

You know you are making progress because you're passing them.

In most recovery meetings, these landmarks are called the 12 Steps. In grace-based recovery, we call these landmarks Mile Markers. God will lead you down His river of grace and, as you grow, He will take you past 12 mile markers that indicate your progress.

That's how you know you are **moving forward**.

These mile markers matter!

Each of these stop-off points help you gain perspective on how you got hooked, and they empower you to stay healthy. Don't blow these 12 mile markers off!

We believe this plan is inspired by God, to help lead you to freedom and a better life.

We want to end this chapter by reminding you one more time of God's great grace to you:

2 Corinthians 12:9 *"My grace is sufficient for you, for my power is made perfect in weakness. Therefore I will boast all the more gladly about my weaknesses, so that Christ's power may rest on me."*

71

If you are going to lead a life of recovery and live it out by teaching it to others, you need to understand that God's grace is all you need.

You don't have to trust your own self-effort to receive freedom.

His grace is sufficient for you.

His power,
His wisdom,
and His strength
will **set you free**.

> His grace is
> sufficient for you.
>
> His power,
> His wisdom,
> and His strength
> will set you free.

So now let's journey down this river of grace and unpack each mile marker.

This is how you can begin to live free from the forces that led to your vice, addiction, or bad habit.

SECTION 3
Flowing Down His River of Grace
(The 12 Mile Markers)

Chapter 7
Admit We Are Powerless

Mile Marker 1:
We admit we are powerless over our vice, addiction, or
bad habit, and our lives are unmanageable.

"There will come a time when you believe
everything is finished. That will be the beginning."

- Louis L'Amour

When a person starts out in recovery, they have generally already hit rock bottom.

Fishermen know that in any lake, river, or reservoir, there is a bottom, and it is rocky sometimes.

For people to pull free of their addiction, vice, or bad habit, they must hit rock bottom and admit that the life they are living is really messed up.

Have you hit rock bottom yet?

The truth is that none of this will work if you're unable to admit that you have hit rock bottom and something needs to change.

Jeremiah 6:14 You can't heal a wound by saying it's not there! (TLB)

Refuse to live in denial about your vice, addiction, or bad habit. Honestly admit you have a problem that you are powerless to handle on your own.

Joe Walsh from the Eagles battled with addiction for over two decades. He wrote a song called "One Day At A Time".

We love the lyrics:

> *Well I finally got around to admit*
> *that I might have a problem.*

But I thought it was just too damn big of a mountain to climb.

Well I got down on my knees and said 'Hey!'
'I just cant go on livin' this way!'
Guess I have to learn to live my life one day at a time. [1]

That is the key. Admit you have a problem and start living one day at a time!

"Well, how do I do that?" you ask.

It is simple. There are two keys to admitting we are powerless.

First, we must get completely honest.

We know that staying in our vices, addictions, and bad habits required us to make up stories to stay addicted and hooked. People who struggle have a difficult time being honest, because somewhere along the line they believed it was okay to get by with a little white lie.

And then addicts
tend to lie
about a lie,
to get out of a lie.

Straight up, a little white lie is still a lie, and not the truth.

When you can honestly look at yourself and say, "Just for today, I am not going to fall into my habit," and at the end of the day remind yourself that you didn't, you have started a new habit called honesty.

When you are having a conversation with someone and catch yourself telling a lie, what if you stopped and told that person that you need to start over and tell them the truth?

Simple little things like this start you in an honest flow of grace.

Speaking of honesty, we will be honest with you here too. We have had relapses.

Sometimes we get re-hooked in our addictions and vices. Bruce and Eric have had this happen several times.

We fall back into our old pattern of behaviors and go back to trying to fix our lives in our own strength, and this messes us up.

The key to staying free is honesty!

We have to tell ourselves and someone else the truth every time we fall back into our old patterns of behavior, and so do you!

You can't hide it, even one time.

Even one lie creates a crack in the foundation of an honest life. Let your sponsor or someone you trust know that you had a slip, but you still want and need their help and support.

Mostly, they probably don't care about the slip as much as they care that you still want to honestly get your life right.

A great verse that has helped us through our first few days of recovery is this:

Proverbs 24:16 *For though a righteous man falls seven times, he rises again...*

Notice, righteousness is not being perfect. Righteousness is just getting back up and moving forward.

In recovery, they say it this way: **NEVER QUIT QUITTING!**

So you messed up one day - who cares?! Just be honest and admit it and start over - ONE DAY AT A TIME!

The second key is commitment.

You have to decide that you are committed to this river of grace and not interested in going back to those old behaviors and temptations.

You have to actually be committed to your own life change.

No one can quit for you.

No one can talk you into this.

You must decide for yourself that you want the new life Christ offers.

Years ago Bruce was leading a recovery meeting, and a blizzard hit Minnesota. At the time, the meeting had about 6-8 people attending and there was some consideration of calling everyone and cancelling the meeting.

> **No one can quit for you.**
> **No one can talk you into this.**
> **You must decide for yourself that you want the new life Christ offers.**

But something (the Holy Spirit) reminded Bruce that recovery is a life of commitment. Just like we used to be committed to going to the bar, the dealer's house, or the casino, whether there was a blizzard or not.

Now we are committed to a **life of freedom and joy**.

We are committed to a **better high than getting high**!

Bruce went to the meeting in the snowstorm, just in case someone might show up. On the drive in, the wind was blowing at forty miles per hour and nine inches of snow had accumulated in the two-hour period before the meeting.

The parking lot wasn't plowed, and it was miserable.

But when he got up to the door, there was a guy standing there (we will call him Jim). He was in the snow with his hood up, smoking a cigarette and listening to tunes on his headphones.

That night, because of Bruce's commitment to a life of recovery, Jim got to experience life change.

He stayed sober for 24 more hours.

That night, Bruce and Jim had one of the greatest meetings ever. Today, Jim has several years of recovery and is thriving at life.

See, this is the commitment that recovery takes, rain, snow, or shine. When you decide to commit to Jesus and His grace, staying sober one day at a time, and attending meetings, you will find recovery.

Will you openly admit you have a problem? Write down your vice, addiction, or bad habit below:

_____

_____

_____

Will you openly admit that your vice, addiction, or bad habit has rendered you powerless?

Say it out loud: I am powerless over _____, and my life has become unmanageable.

Will you go and tell someone else that statement openly? (Tell your spouse, friend, or family member the HONEST truth about your situation and what is going on with you.)

Will you go to a recovery meeting?

Find a local meeting in your area and attend, openly and honestly admitting you have a problem you are powerless to conquer in your own strength.

Will you commit to yourself, God, and another person not to "use" for the next 24 hours? Recovery happens 24 hours at a time, sometimes 24 seconds at a time.

Just like you were committed every day to the bad habit of alcohol or porn, commit for the next 24 hours to avoid your vice.

Don't commit to longer than 24 hours.

Recovery happens **one day at a time**.

Write out a prayer thanking God for the power He will give you to get through the next 24 hours.

_____

_____

_____

_____

_____

_____

_____

_____

_____

_____

_____

_____

[1]*Walsh, Joe. "One Day At A Time" Lyrics. Analog Man*
Fantasy Records/Concord Music Group, 2012.

Chapter 8
Came to Believe

Mile Marker 2:
Came to believe that Jesus and the
power of His grace is the only thing
that can free me and restore me to sanity.

"And I came to believe in a power much higher than I,
I came to believe that I needed help to get by,
In childlike faith I gave in and gave him a try,
And I came to believe in a power much higher than I."
- Johnny Cash

Mile Marker 2 is about replacing your natural powerlessness with a supernatural power source.

It is about coming to believe that maybe Jesus is more powerful than your vice, addiction, or bad habit, and that His power can free you and **restore your sanity**.

We think one of the most beautiful verses about recovery in the whole Bible was written by the Apostle Paul.

1 Corinthians 10:13 There isn't any temptation that you have experienced which is unusual for humans. God, who faithfully keeps his promises, will not allow you to be tempted beyond your power to resist. But when you are tempted, he will also give you the ability to endure the temptation as your way of escape. (GWT)

Did you see the two key phrases in that verse?

[God] will not allow you to be tempted beyond your power to resist.

God is watching out for you!

When you come to believe, He won't let temptation be more powerful than His power **in you.**

Just like a good parent watches our for their kids, God the Good Parent is watching out for you! You have the power to conquer temptation when you come to believe this!

...he will also give you the ability to endure...
Notice, when you come to believe, He gives you supernatural endurance. You now possess a power you did not have before!

Before...

...you would see the liquor store and have to stop.
Now you can endure.

...you would see the casino sign and have to go in.
Now you can pass it by.

...you would see the ad for the porn site and have to click it.
Now you are stronger than that, and can turn away.

Believe you were given this **power!**

To help you understand Mile Marker 2, we need to use a couple Bible stories as a backdrop.

Story # 1:

There was this man who had been paralyzed for thirty-eight years. Just imagine that!

For thirty-eight years, he had been living in his broken condition, unable to heal himself.

Then along came Jesus and His powerful grace.

Check out what happened.

John 5:1-11 Some time later, Jesus went up to Jerusalem for one of the Jewish festivals. Now there is in Jerusalem near the Sheep Gate a pool, which in Aramaic is called Bethesda and which is surrounded by five covered colonnades. Here a great number of disabled people used to lie—the blind, the lame, the paralyzed. One who was there had been an invalid for thirty-eight years.

When Jesus saw him lying there and learned that he had been in this condition for a long time, he asked him, "<u>Do you want to get well?</u>" "Sir," the invalid replied, "I have no one to help me into the pool when the water is stirred. While I am trying to get in, someone else goes down ahead of me." Then Jesus said to him, "Get up! Pick up your mat and walk." <u>At once the man was cured</u>; he picked up his mat and walked.

We want to ask you the same question Jesus asked this man.

"Do you want to get well?"

Of course you do! This man felt as though everyone else was getting the help they needed, but that he was always overlooked.

But then Jesus saw him, and spoke healing over him. Notice the words in verse 11: *"AT ONCE the man was cured."*

> **Jesus wants you to know that you don't have to sit there feeling hopeless.**
>
> **You are not alone - He notices you!**

Jesus wants you to know that you don't have to sit there feeling hopeless.

You are not alone - He notices you!

You are never overlooked by God!

When you give your life to Jesus, you have to power to GET UP AND WALK!

You will be
immediately,
completely,
totally,
AT ONCE,
healed.

This man, after thirty-eight years of brokenness, **came to believe** that Jesus and the power of His grace was the only thing that could free him from being paralyzed and restore sanity to his life again.

What if you came to believe as well?
What if you gave up trying everything else you've tried to get well and did what this man did?

Will you give Jesus a chance?

Let us share a second story with you.

The Gospel of Mark tells the story of a woman who had been bleeding for twelve years. She had gone to doctor after doctor to try and find healing, but she was powerless to change herself!

Story # 2:

Mark 5:24-30 *A woman in the crowd had suffered for twelve years with constant bleeding. She had suffered a great deal from many doctors, and over the years she had spent everything she had to pay them, but she had gotten no better. In fact, she had gotten worse.*

She had heard about Jesus, so she came up behind him through the crowd and touched his robe. For she thought to herself, "If I can just touch his robe, I will be healed." Immediately the bleeding stopped, and she could feel in her body that she had been healed of her terrible condition. (NLT)

Notice what this woman thought: *"If I can just touch his robe, I will be healed."*

This woman **came to believe** that a power greater than herself could restore her to sanity, she saw that power in Jesus, and BAM!

Look at the word that is used in verse 29: **IMMEDIATELY** the bleeding stopped and the healing began, all because of the power of Jesus and His grace.

See, something happens **IMMEDIATELY**
when you **COME TO BELIEVE**.

Now let's ask some questions:

To you, who is Jesus?

_____

Read the following verses and write down what they mean to you. As you read, ask God to help you come to believe.

John 14:6 _Jesus told him, "I am the way, the truth, and the life. No one can come to the Father except through me." (NLT)_

What does that mean to you?

_____

_____

_____

Romans 10:9-10 _If you confess with your mouth that Jesus is Lord and believe in your heart that God raised him from the dead, you will be saved. For it is by believing in your heart that you are made right with God, and it is by confessing with your mouth that you are saved. (NLT)_

What does this say to you?

_____

_____

_____

2 Corinthians 5:17 *Anyone who belongs to Christ has become a new person. The old life is gone; a new life has begun! (NLT)*

What does this say to you?

_____

_____

_____

Revelation 3:20 *"Look! I stand at the door and knock. If you hear my voice and open the door, I will come in, and we will share a meal together as friends." (NLT)*
What does this say to you?

_____

_____

After looking at those verses, are you ready to give your life to Jesus?

Do you have the faith to say, "I came to believe?"

Now, maybe you are not ready to say that yet.

That is ok.

We want to give you one more verse of scripture to consider. One time Jesus encountered a man who was asking for a miracle. His son was possessed by an evil spirit, and the man was begging for Jesus to heal his boy.

Look at the dialogue that follows:

Mark 9:23-24 *[Jesus said], "All things are possible for one who believes." Immediately the boy's father cried out and said, "I believe; help my unbelief!" (ESV)*

Notice the boy's father wanted to believe.

He sort of believed.

He was desperate for a miracle.

It was hard to really believe, so he even asked for help believing!

It is okay for you to ask for help believing.

Maybe you want to come to believe in Jesus, but believing is difficult for you.
We understand. You have been through so much pain and disappointment, it is hard to believe.

Ask God for help.

Pray something like this:

Jesus Christ, I want to believe in You. I want to believe that You are the only power greater than myself that can restore me to sanity.

I ask You for the power to believe in You right now.

Give me the supernatural ability to overcome my disbelief. From this moment on I will believe that Jesus and His grace is the only power that can restore me to sanity.

Write that prayer for yourself:

_____

_____

_____

_____

_____

_____

_____

_____

_____

_____

_____

_____

_____

_____

_____

_____

_____

_____

_____

_____

_____

Now we're ready to move on and experience the rest of the mile markers! Let's keep going in the flow!

Chapter 9
Turn Our Lives Over

Mile Marker 3:
We turned our will and our lives
over to the care of Jesus and His grace!

"Only through repentance and faith in Christ can anyone
be saved. No religious activity will be sufficient, only
true faith in Jesus Christ alone."

- Ravi Zacharias

As pastors, we've had the blessing of leading thousands of people to Jesus, but the most important person we could ever talk to is you.

Right now.

In this moment.

Us. This book.

You. God.

If you are still reading, God has you at a pivotal point in your life. He is about to take you across the line of faith into a new and better life.

The day you choose to turn your will and life over to the care of Jesus and His grace is the most amazing day in your personal history.

Just like the day a person gets married, baptized, or has a baby,

**you will never forget the day
you give your life to Jesus.**

Later in life, you will share with your loved ones about the moment when you got on a knee and said, "Jesus, I believe in you. I believe You are God and died for me. Forgive my sins and lead my life, take me to heaven when I die."

In that moment, you gain entrance into a relationship with your Creator in heaven for all of eternity.

This is what we believe, and that's what this mile marker is all about. We completely surrender our own self-will and all areas of our life over to the care of Jesus and His grace.

For me (Bruce), this happened on a set of railroad tracks.

After being sober for about three months, I was attending recovery meetings regularly and working a rigid recovery program. I was calling my sponsor (mentor) pretty much everyday.

Then one day my sponsor gave me a challenge.

*He said, "Now that you have some length of sobriety, I want you to go **make your peace with God**."*

This was a pretty big deal.

I knew that at some point someone was going to talk to me about the God thing. I grew up going to church, but couldn't stand feeling forced to go.

Every Sunday, my mom would play country music to wake me up, excited to go to church. There were times I believed God must exist, but I didn't think He had anything to do with me. Therefore, I didn't really want to have anything to do with the whole God or church thing.

A few days after I received this instruction, I got in my truck and drove down to where I used to get high and drunk with some of my neighborhood buddies.

I brought my dog with me and was throwing a hunting dummy for him. I was really reluctant to go through with this "making peace with God" ordeal.

*But I was **trying to do this right**.*

I went to this perfect spot, where only a few months earlier I had been plastered, and dropped to a knee.

There was snow everywhere.

It was cold and the sun was just about to set.

I said my **first authentic prayer** *to Jesus and said, "Okay God, if you're so 'blankety-blank' real, then I dare you to show up in my life. Amen." Then I got up and walked back to my truck.*

Driving home, I actually felt pretty good about the whole thing and was excited to tell my sponsor I had done what I had to do to make my peace with God.

I popped in a Metallica CD and cranked up the song "Enter Sandman". As that song was jamming pretty good and loud, I heard God's response to my prayer on the railroad tracks.

God spoke.

We want to push the pause button for a second in the middle of this story and tell you that we believe that God speaks to us.

Not audibly, but to our spirit.

He speaks with a still, small voice to our souls and,
when we listen,
we will hear Him talking.

So this is what I thought I heard God say:

"If you want to know Me, then I dare you to go home and dust off that book that your mom gave you twenty years ago.

You know the one?

It's My book, called the Bible.

I'd like you to open it.

Read it.

This is how you'll know Me."

Like most guys, I love a good challenge. So I drove home as fast as I could.

I ran in the house and found My Bible. I didn't really know where to start, so I just opened to any old random page.

Pause.

This is not necessarily the sort of passage that God will use for you, but it's exactly what Bruce needed to hear when he was where he was at the time.

Un-pause.

Here's what I read:

Galatians 5:16-21 *So I say, live by the Spirit and you will not gratify the desires of the sinful nature. For the sinful nature desires what is contrary to the Spirit. And the Spirit desires what is contrary to the sinful nature. They are in conflict with each other so that you do not do what you want. But if you are led by the Spirit, you are not under the law [of Moses].*

The acts of the sinful nature are obvious; sexual immorality, impurity, debauchery, idolatry, witchcraft, hatred, discord, jealousy, fits of rage, selfish ambition, dissensions, factions, envy, drunkenness, wild parties, and the like. I warn you, as I did before, that those who live like this will not inherit the kingdom of God.

Right after reading this,
I dropped my Bible on the floor
***and cried**.*

I knew as I read through that list of wrongs, I was all of those things. I had heard about heaven, and if heaven was real, I definitely wanted to go there instead of the other place.

I told myself that there had to be more to this story than, "If I live like this, I'm not going to heaven." So I picked my Bible back up and continued reading.

The next part of this passage is what changed me forever.

Galatians 5:22-24 *But the fruit of the Spirit is love, joy, peace, patience, kindness, goodness, faithfulness, gentleness, and self-control. Against such things there is no law [only grace]. Those who belong to Christ Jesus have crucified the sinful nature with its passions and desires. Since we live by the Spirit, let us keep in step with the Spirit.*

After reading that, I buckled.

I recognized that I was all of those things that were sin-related, but wanted all of what the Spirit offered me in verses 22-24.

I didn't hesitate.

I bent a knee all over again and asked Jesus Christ to be my Forgiver, Leader, and Lord.

> **God took a washed-up, drunken fisherman and made him a sober fisher of men.**

I was IMMEDIATELY transformed.

God took a washed-up, drunken fisherman and made him a sober fisher of men.

Eric's story with Mile Marker 3 is just as radical.

I (Eric) grew up in a strict, religious home and church where God came across (at least to me) as a strict, cosmic cop.

He was the God of rules, and I just knew if I stepped out of line, He was going to throw lightning bolts at me.

By the time I was in tenth grade,
I was pretty sick of the whole
God of rules,
religion,
jump-through-hoops-to-make-God-happy thing.

*So I moved on to **full-on rebellion against God**.*

I wanted nothing to do with this uptight, heavy-handed, mean-spirited religion.

This rebellion against God led to full-on rebellion against my parents. My dad and I had some pretty epic fights and could hardly stand to be in the same room at times.

In desperation, he took me on a road trip to New York State to go camping in the Adirondack Mountains.

One night around a campfire,
I got to talking with a Christian.

This guy seemed different.

He shared his story with me. He had been a car thief and had become a Christian in prison. To this day, I still can't remember his name or even what we talked about most that night.

But I can remember the statement God used to change my life forever.

This man said,
"Don't you know that God is
about a relationship with you?

He is **not about a list of rules**."
I had grown up in church, and that was the first time I had
ever heard that.

This man went on to say that God was about walking and
talking and doing life with me exactly as I am, with no
judgment.

God wanted a friendship with me!

That statement blasted into my heart like a thousand drums
inside a phone booth.

All kinds of thoughts swirled in my brain:

What if this was the truth?

What if God really likes me the way I am?

What if He isn't just on an agenda to change me, but is out to
do life with me?

What if I can have a relationship with God?

What if God would talk to me and is **not mad at me?**

Eventually I knew that what this man was telling me was right
and true.

I could feel it in my heart.

I gave in.

I got down on my knees in the dirt by that campfire and a
prayer something like this:

"God, if you are really real, and you really want to have a
relationship with me, I give you my life. I dare you to talk to
me and change me and help me. Forgive me for fighting you.

Today I trust you.

Jesus Christ, I make you my Savior and my God. Amen."
*I got up from the dirt **different**.*

*I don't know how to explain it, but **everything changed**.*

God started talking,
and empowering me,
and helping me and
my life radically changed for the better.

What if you did the same thing right now?

What if you, like Eric and Bruce, not only came to believe, but also turned your will and your ways over to the care of Jesus and His grace?

All it takes for you is to say this prayer from a heart that truly means it.

You can do it wherever you'd like. If you need to get by a campfire like Eric or on some railroad tracks like Bruce, go for it, but make sure there's not a train coming.

Just bend a knee and pray this:

Jesus Christ, I believe You are God and that You died for me. I am sorry for blowing You off. Forgive me of all my sin. I ask You to be the Leader of my life. Take me to heaven when I die. I will trust You and follow You. In Jesus' name I pray. Amen."

If you just said that prayer for the first time, let us be the first to congratulate you and tell you that there is a huge party that just started in heaven on your behalf!

All of heaven is in party mode, and the angels are hanging a "Welcome Home (INSERT YOUR NAME HERE)" banner above the entrance of heaven in your honor!

Here is how the Bible describes that celebration:

Luke 15:10 *Likewise, I say to you, there is joy in the presence of the angels of God over one sinner who repents. (NKJV)*

The angels are throwing a party because you turned your will and way over to Jesus!

Well done!

There is one more part to Mile Marker 3.

Let's think about fishing again for a second.

When we catch a great fish, we take pictures, we high-five and celebrate! We text those pictures to our friends or call our mom just to brag for a second.

We think you need to do the same thing with "turning your will and life over to the care of Jesus and His grace."

Someone else needs to celebrate this with you. Who do you know that has been praying for you for a long time to finally commit and follow Jesus?

Write their name here: _____

Now we want you to call them or text them and tell them this: "Today I decided to turn my will and life over to the care of Jesus and His grace. Today I made Jesus the Forgiver and Leader of my life. I follow Christ now."

Go for it!

Make the call.

Send the text.

Your friend or family member wants to celebrate this great moment with you!

This is the **biggest decision of your life**.

This determines your eternal destiny.

103

You don't ever want to forget this moment.

Take a moment to write the story of why you decided to follow Jesus.

What happened? Where were you? When was it, and how did you celebrate, because you made Jesus Christ your Forgiver and Leader:

_____

_____

_____

_____

_____

_____

_____

_____

_____

_____

_____

_____

_____

_____

_____

_____

_____

_____

Now you're ready to float down the river of grace to Mile Marker 4!

Chapter 10
Fearless Moral Inventory

Mile Marker 4:
We examined ourselves and the root causes that
led us to our vices, addictions and bad habits.

"What lies behind us and what lies before us are small
matters compared to what lies within us."

- Ralph Waldo Emerson

Back when I (Eric) was in high school, I went with some friends to the Boundary Water Canoe Area Wilderness for a week-long fishing trip.

I was new to the whole fishing scene, and the only lure I knew to fish with at the time was a Rapala Shad Rap.

These lures were expensive for a high school kid with limited money, so I bought five lures and went on the trip.

Fishing was great.

One afternoon we were below a waterfall hammering the northern and walleye with white and black shad raps.

Then the unthinkable happened.

I snagged my Shad Rap on the bottom of the lake. I tried everything to pull it up, but it wouldn't come loose.

In desperation, I stripped down to my boxer shorts and went in over the side of the boat to retrieve my lure. I followed the line down to the bottom, grabbed hold of the lure, and pulled.

The hooks still would not come loose!

I felt around on the bottom, and determined the lure was caught on an old burlap bag.

I swam back to the surface and told my friend Tim, "My lure is stuck on a weird squishy burlap bag down on the bottom!"

Tim replied, "Well pull the bag up, and I will get your lure."

I was like, "NO WAY! That bag is super gross and I don't know what's in it!"

But Tim kept pestering me, so I dove down deep again.

This time I grabbed the bag with both hands and pushed off the bottom. Slowly, I started to haul it to the surface. I struggled to swim up and, finally, I grabbed the side of the boat with one hand. I pulled up the bag in the other hand.

Tim shouted, "IT STINKS!"

I shouted back, "I told you it's SQUISHY and heavy!"

I was really starting to freak out.

"Get the lure!" I hollered.

Tim grabbed a knife and cut the lure free. I dropped the bag immediately, too freaked out to look inside.

To this day, I wonder what was in that bag!

Was it a decomposing body?

Was it sunken treasure?

If only I had kept the bag and looked inside, but it was just too scary!

We tell you this story because this is basically what Mile Marker 4 is like. You need to dive down deep into your past and pull up all the old, smelly, squishy, burlap bags in your life to cut them loose and throw them away.

You need to **deal with the stuff** that's deep in your past **that scares you the most**.

We know this is not necessarily easy; it wasn't for us.

Think of this mile marker as the river rapids on the journey of grace. If you deal with stuff honestly and completely, and make it thorough, you will experience a freedom like never before.

So, grab and pen and let's go diving for burlap bags!

Let's see what internal junk we can find to get rid of in our hearts.

Lamentations 3:40 *Let us examine our ways and test them, and let us return to the Lord.*

God wants you to dive in and examine your heart to see what is there. We are going to go diving for five things: Our resentments, fears, sexual misconducts, negative emotions, and finally, gratitudes.

INSTRUCTIONS FOR COMPLETING MILE MARKER 4

For each section below, read the Bible verses, then fill out the charts as honestly and completely as you can.

Here are some tips for you as you complete Mile Marker 4:

1. You may wish to use a separate notebook for your Mile Marker 4 lists to allow yourself enough room to process.

2. Carry a pad of Post-It Notes with you for a few days. Remember, you are trying to bring to the surface your resentments, fears, sexual misconducts, and negative emotions. This way you can deal with them and move forward. Write down names or situations on the Post-It Notes as you think of them throughout the day and keep them in your pocket or somewhere safe.

3. This process will probably take you a week or two. Try not to get frustrated if you don't get it all done in a day.

4. At the end of each day, transfer the names/memories from your Post-It Notes onto your list and add the details in as needed.

5. Once you're finished and ready for Mile Marker 5, you will tear the pages your lists are on right out of this book. Feel free to write all over them!

6. If you don't know whether or not to write something down, do it anyway. It is best not to leave any burlap bags behind!

Now you can begin.

My Resentments

Job 5:2 *Surely resentment destroys the fool... (NLT)*

Resentment never destroys the other person, it only destroys yourself.

Holding on to resentment against other people is like drinking poison and hoping the other person dies.

It never works.

You have to let your resentments go in order to get free and move on to a better life.

Job 36:13 *For the godless are full of resentment. (NLT)*

If your will and life are turned over to Christ, you are full of Christ and have no room for resentment.

Unbelievers are filled with bitterness and anger toward others. Believers empty that out and fill themselves with the love of Christ.

Let all those resentments go.

Ephesians 4:31-32 *Get rid of all bitterness, rage, anger, harsh words, and slander, as well as all types of evil behavior. Instead, be kind to each other, tenderhearted, forgiving one another, just as God through Christ has forgiven you. (NLT)*

Do you see the reason you can let your resentments go?

Jesus has no resentments toward you.

He forgave you for all your mistakes, and asks you to do the same for others.

Resentment is like a rubber band on your heart that keeps getting tighter and tighter. It is slowly cutting off more and more of the circulation to your joy, peace, and happiness.

Let that stuff go so you can **enjoy your life again!**

On the following pages, we have provided instructions and a chart for honestly listing your resentments and releasing yourself to God and His love for you.

Instructions:

Column 1: Who/what am I resentful at?
- Here you will write down a word or name for each resentment.
- Example: My Brother

Column 2: Describe the resentment.
- Here you will write down a triggering word or two that will help you remember what your resentment is.
- Example: He ate the last piece of pizza.

Column 3: What this affects.
- Here you will write down what this resentment affects in your life. Here is a list of things your resentments can affect: relationships, ambitions, self-esteem, or security. It is important to write this down so you can verbalize later that your life has been affected.
- Example: When my brother ate the last piece of pizza, it affected our relationship because it broke trust.

Column 4: Pause for prayer.
- Take a minute to say a prayer for each of the people/things you write down.
- Example: *God, I ask that You remove my resentment for my brother. I pray that You will give me a new and purposeful heart to show Your love to him. Make me into the person that You designed me to be. In Jesus' name. Amen.*

Column 5: My part.
- At this time, you will be examining yourself. Honestly ask yourself what part you played in the resentment. Were you selfish (this is mine), self-seeking (it is yours, but I want it), dishonest, frightened, prideful, jealous, divisive, full of rage, envious, was this your God (idol)? As you see your part, write down each word that describes it so you can share your side later.
- Example: I was selfish because I wanted that last piece of pizza and didn't want anyone else to have it. I yelled at my brother and said something I shouldn't have said.

Column 6: Forgiveness.
- It is extraordinarily helpful, as you go through each item on each list, to ask if you need to seek forgiveness from God, yourself, or others. Also write down who you need to forgive along the way so you can offer that to Jesus in Mile Marker 5.
- Example: I will ask for forgiveness from my brother because I yelled at him, and that was wrong. Then I will forgive him for eating the pizza without asking my permission.

Use the charts on the next couple of pages to write down your resentments.

	Resentment 1	Resentment 2	Resentment 3	Resentment 4	Resentment 5
Who/What					
Describe the Resentment					
What This Affects					
Prayer					
My Part					
Forgiveness					

	Resentment 6	Resentment 7	Resentment 8	Resentment 9	Resentment 10
Who/What					
Describe the Resentment					
What This Affects					
Prayer					
My Part					
Forgiveness					

My Fears

1 John 4:18 There is no fear in love. But perfect love drives out fear...

God loves you perfectly.

You don't have to be afraid anymore.

2 Timothy 1:7 For God has not given us a spirit of fear, but of power and of love and of a sound mind. (NKJV)

God does not wish for you to live with your fears.

He wants to give you
power

to overcome them,
love to drive them out,
and wisdom to **leave them behind**.

We have provided instructions and a chart for honestly listing your fears and releasing yourself to God and His love for you.

Instructions:

Column 1: Who/what is my fear?
- Here you will write down each of your fears.
- Example: Fear of failing.

Column 2: Describe the fear.
- Here you will write down why you are afraid.
- Example: Don't want to let people down.

Column 3: What this affects.
- Here you will write down what this fear affects in your life. Here is a list of things your fears can affect: relationships, ambitions, self-esteem, or security. It is important to write this down so you can verbalize later that your life has been affected.

- Example: This fear affects my ambitions because I'm afraid to try new things. It also affects my self-esteem because I am really hard on myself when I fail.

Column 4: Pause for prayer.
- Take a minute to say a prayer for each of the fears you wrote down, or each of the people you are afraid of.
- Example: *God, remove my fear of failure. I give You now control of my life, and pray that Your will be done with me. This fear is not from You, so I leave it at the foot of your cross and offer the rest of me to You. In Jesus' name. Amen.*

Column 5: My part.
- At this time, you will be examining yourself. Honestly ask yourself what part you played in the fear. Were you selfish (this is mine), self-seeking (it is yours, but I want it), dishonest, prideful, jealous, divisive, full of rage, envious, was this your God (idol)? As you see your part, write down each word that describes it so you can share your side later.
- Example: I have allowed this fear to control my behavior and hold me back. I made an idol of succeeding.

Column 6: Forgiveness.
- It is extraordinarily helpful, as you go through each item on each list, to ask if you need to seek forgiveness from God, yourself, or others. Also write down who you need to forgive along the way so you can offer that to Jesus in Mile Marker 5.
- Example: I will ask God to forgive me for not trusting that He loves me, despite my failures. I will forgive myself for not trying new things because I was afraid of failing.

Use the charts on the next couple of pages to write down your fears.

	Fear 1	Fear 2	Fear 3	Fear 4	Fear 5
Who/What					
Describe the Fear					
What This Affects					
Prayer					
My Part					
Forgiveness					

	Fear 6	Fear 7	Fear 8	Fear 9	Fear 10
Who/What					
Describe the Fear					
What This Affects					
Prayer					
My Part					
Forgiveness					

Sexual Misconduct

1 Corinthians 6:18-20 Run from sexual sin! No other sin so clearly affects the body as this one does. For sexual immorality is a sin against your own body. Don't you realize that your body is the temple of the Holy Spirit, who lives in you and was given to you by God? You do not belong to yourself, for God bought you with a high price. So you must honor God with your body. (NLT)

Sexual misconduct is the area where most people have the biggest regrets.

> **The good news is, God PAID A HIGH PRICE FOR YOU!**
>
> **He gave His life as payment for every sexual misdeed.**

Something about sex outside of God's plan hurts us deeply.

The good news is, GOD PAID A HIGH PRICE FOR YOU!

He gave His life as payment for every sexual misdeed.

Now you can use your body appropriately because Christ has cut the line to this temptation.

Job 31:1 "I made a covenant with my eyes not to look lustfully at a young woman."

If sexual sin is a struggle in your life, we encourage you to memorize this verse.

If a pretty person walks by you, and you're tempted to look again, you can remind yourself, "Nope, I have made a covenant with my eyes not to look at them sexually!"

We have provided instructions and a chart for honestly listing your sexual misconducts and releasing yourself to God and His love for you.

Instructions:

Column 1: Who/what was my sexual misconduct?
- Here you will write down each of your sexual misconducts.
- Example: Jane Doe

Column 2: Describe the misconduct.
- Here you will write down what the misconduct was.
- Example: We had a one-night stand while we were drunk.

Column 3: What this affects.
- Here you will write down what this misconduct affects in your life. Here is a list of things your sexual misconducts can affect: relationships, ambitions, self-esteem, or security. It is important to write this down so you can verbalize later that your life has been affected.
- Example: This one-night stand affects my current relationship because they don't know the truth.

Column 4: Pause for prayer.
- Take a minute to say a prayer for each of the people/misconducts you wrote down.
- Example: *God, please forgive me for my sexual misconduct with Jane Doe. I pray for Jane and ask that You bless her life. I pray that she will be healthy and strong and thrive in this area of her life, and I ask that You would do the same with me. In Jesus' name. Amen.*

Column 5: My part.
- At this time, you will be examining yourself. Honestly ask yourself what part you played in the misconduct. Were you selfish (this is mine), self-seeking (it is yours, but I want it), frightened, dishonest, prideful, jealous, divisive, full of rage, envious, was this your God (idol)? As you see your part, write down each word that describes it so you can share your side later.
- Example: Jane is a child of God and not my wife. Taking advantage of her and thinking only of my own desires was self-seeking and wrong.

Column 6: Forgiveness.

- It is extraordinarily helpful, as you go through each item on each list, to ask if you need to seek forgiveness from God, yourself, or others. Also write down who you need to forgive along the way so you can offer that to Jesus in Mile Marker 5.

- Example: I will ask Jane for forgiveness because I took advantage of her. I will forgive myself for doing the wrong thing. (Side note: We seek forgiveness from others during Mile Marker 9. Please don't move forward with this until you have spoken with your guide/sponsor and determined if this is the best course of action.)

Use the charts on the next couple of pages to write down your sexual misconducts.

	Misconduct 1	Misconduct 2	Misconduct 3	Misconduct 4	Misconduct 5
Who/What					
Describe the Misconduct					
What This Affects					
Prayer					
My Part					
Forgiveness					

	Misconduct 6	Misconduct 7	Misconduct 8	Misconduct 9	Misconduct 10
Who/What					
Describe the Misconduct					
What This Affects					
Prayer					
My Part					
Forgiveness					

Negative Emotions

We understand that what you just went through to write all this junk down took a lot of courage and time.

You probably had some deep emotions as a result of the spiritual surgery you just went through.

We'd like to suggest that you take a look at the emotions that affected you as you went through this process.

Circle all that apply:

Hurt
Angry
Frustrated
Guilty
Shameful
Embarrassed
Bitter
Grief
Despair
Depressed
Hatred
Other _____

We know these emotions can really impede our progress, so we'd like help you deal with all these feelings in a positive way.

Think of your life like a cup.

Right now, you may be filled with all kinds of negative emotions. When your cup is full of negativity, you can't fill up on the **joy and hope of life**.

Before you can be full of joy, you must empty out the sorrows and hurts of life. If you circled any of the negative emotions we listed, we'd like to help you pour out these emotions to God by offering up a simple prayer.

Let's ask God to heal each of these emotions for you.

Psalm 142:1-2 *I cry out to the Lord; I plead for the Lord's mercy. I pour out my complaints before him and tell him all my troubles. (NLT)*

Do it.

Pour out your emotions to Him. Read/pray this aloud, and do it once for each emotion. Pour it all out and then lift your cup to Jesus to fill.

Fill in the blanks of the emotions you experienced as you walk through this prayer:

Jesus Christ, I am filled up with the emotion of

_____.

This happened because...

_____

_____

_____

_____

I now recognize that I must empty this negative emotion and carry it no longer.

I confess the sin of _____
(list the negative emotion).

I ask You to forgive me for feeling this way. I release this emotion and in Jesus' name, I break all agreements in all levels and all dimensions with the negative emotion of

_____.
Right now I ask You, Jesus Christ, to replace my negative feelings with Your joy and peace.

128

I believe that I am free of this negative emotion and that my cup is empty so that You can fill me with Your love, hope, and power.

In Jesus' name. Amen!

With each negative emotion, pray this prayer, and watch as God empties your cup and fills it with joy!

David says this in the Bible:

Psalm 23:5 ...*my cup overflows.*

Your cup will overflow with
joy
and
hope
and
peace
once you pour out all those negative emotions to God.

Take a few deep breaths and exhale with a smile.

We hope you are really beginning to feel Jesus setting you free!

Gratitude

Psalm 118:24 This is the day the LORD has made. We will rejoice and be glad in it. (NLT)

Every day you can decide to find something to be grateful for.

There is someone that loves you.

There is a possession you own that brings you joy.

There is a possibility in the future that excites you.

There is a past memory that fills you with happiness.

If you *decide* to rejoice today, **you will rejoice.**

Philippians 3:13 ...one thing I do: Forgetting what is behind and straining toward what is ahead...

The past is the past.

You can't change it, but you can have a better future.

> **The past is the past.**
>
> **You can't change it, but you can have a better future.**

Focus on the great future you are going to have once you get free of all these resentments, fears, and past sexual misconducts.

1 Thessalonians 5:18 ...give thanks in ALL circumstances; for this is God's will for you in Christ Jesus.

You have something you can give thanks for today.

In ALL circumstances, you can be grateful.

List the things you are grateful for.

Chapter 11
Admit to God & Others

Mile Marker 5:
We admit to ourselves, another person, and Jesus the exact nature of our wrongs and throw ourselves into Christ's mercy and grace.

"Confession of errors is like a broom which sweeps away the dirt and leaves the surface brighter and clearer. I feel stronger for confession."
- Mahatma Gandhi

When you completed Mile Marker 4, you moved through the smaller rapids on the river of grace. Now you are on to the most serious set of rapids on the river.

When you have finished navigating Mile Marker 5, you will experience a
greater level of
peace,
joy, and
accomplishment
than ever before.

Once again, this mile marker is not easy, but it is so WORTH IT!

It's time to admit the truth of everything that you wrote down in Mile Marker 4 to Jesus and another person you trust.

We want to explain two important verses of scripture before you pass by this mile marker. Here is the first:

1 John 1:9 *If we confess our sins he is faithful and just, he will forgive us our sins and purify us from all unrighteousness.*

This verse says that if we will be open and honest in admitting our sins to God, **HE WILL FORGIVE US!**

That is good news.

If we want to be free of all the things we wrote down in Mile Marker 4, we must confess them to God.

This means you'll want to go through each individual fear, resentment, and sexual misconduct and confess it all to God.

Like this:

Jesus Christ, I confess to You the fear of _____, insecurity of _____, or sexual misconduct with _____.

I acknowledge that I did the wrong thing.

I ask You to forgive me now in the name of Jesus Christ. Wash me clean me with the blood You shed on the cross and remember my sins no more.

I also break all agreements I made with the sin of _____, the fear of _____, the insecurity of _____, and the sexual misconduct with _____.

In Jesus' name, I break all agreements I have made with these spirits on all levels and in all dimensions and command Satan, his servants, their works and effects to leave me alone regarding this issue.

I am free in Christ!

I believe the truth that I am loved and forgiven and that my past and all soul-ties to this event are forever broken. From this moment on, I walk with a new heart that is able to do what is right and honor God.

In Jesus' name. Amen.

We want you to pray this prayer for each and every thing you wrote down in Mile Marker 4.

Yes, really! Each and every one.

However, we do not want you to do this alone. That brings us to the second key verse for Mile Marker 5.

James 5:16 *Therefore confess your sins to each other and pray for each other so that you may be healed.*

Notice that healing happens not only because you confessed your sins, but because you confessed your sins to ANOTHER PERSON!

Something supernatural happens when you open up to another person about the darkness of your life.

> **Something supernatural happens when you open up to another person about the darkness of your life.**

We know sitting down with someone and Jesus to talk about all of the embarrassing truths about ourselves can be difficult and scary, but **it doesn't have to be!**

The people that have actually reached this mile marker are the ones that we've seen experience long-term recovery.

Many times when people pull back and drop an anchor instead of going forward past this marker, it leads them back to addiction.

Something about going through this tough process releases you of the
deep hurt,
baggage,
guilt,
and pain
that is **buried in your soul.**

Because this process is so difficult for so many people, we want to give you some tips for how to pass this mile marker well.

1. Do this with a spiritual leader, not just anyone.

We suggest you call your sponsor, pastor, priest, or spiritual mentor and ask to schedule a time to meet with them to share your resentments, fears, sexual misconducts, emotional baggage, and any other character flaws you need to deal with.

2. Plan on this mile marker taking at least 3-5 hours.

When Eric went through this, it took half of a day of confessing, praying, weeping, and getting free. For Bruce it took even longer - seventeen hours to get through all that he had written down. Plan on taking some real time. If you didn't do the real work in writing anything down in Mile Marker 4, then Mile Marker 5 won't mean anything. Do the real digging you need to do so the transformation you need actually occurs.

3. Only do this with someone of the same gender.

Something about this process is deeply bonding, so adding sexual temptation to it will ruin the honesty that is required.

4. When you meet, make sure you are alone and won't be disturbed for the whole time you need.

5. Invite Jesus into the room and start to go through each of the items you wrote down.

6. Here is an example of how to share one of your resentments, fears, sexual misconduct or emotions:

"So, I have a resentment against my friend (column 1), because he stole my fishing pole (column 2). It affects my: emotions, personal relations, self-esteem, security (column 3), and my part in it is that I have been selfish because…, self-seeking because…, dishonest because…, and frightened because…"

In each case, share as much as you need to.

Tell every story you need to share, get it all out, and deal with it honestly.

Then move onto the next thing you wrote down.

7. Share your resentments first, then your fears, sexual misconducts, and your negative emotions. End with your gratitude list.

8. If you're on the listening end, it's important to pray beforehand and simply listen.

Take notes as needed, and pay attention to special areas that need additional counsel later. But now is just a time to listen.

Be mindful that this person has taken a great deal of time to put these lists together and they have gone to a great deal of effort to be in the room with you.

Your role is to be there with a listening ear and a prayer.

9. End with a final prayer of gratitude to God for His forgiveness and grace.

10. Solidify the significance of this event by burning or tearing up your lists. (We made it easy for you to tear them right out of this book. Remind yourself that God remembers your sins no more! (Isaiah 43:25)

Congratulations! You made it through the toughest rapids on the river of grace, but don't quit yet!

Immediately after completing Mile Marker 5, move to Mile Marker 6. These are designed to be experienced together!

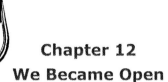

Chapter 12
We Became Open

Mile Marker 6:
We became open for Jesus to
remove our defects of character.

"The same Jesus who turned water into wine can
transform your home, your life, your family, and your
future. He is still in the miracle-working business, and
His business is the business of transformation."

- Adrian Rogers

If we were to summarize this mile marker with a few short words, it would be to get quiet and reflect.

Think about what just happened when you shared all the secrets of your burlap bag of the past with God and another person.

Being alone in quiet reflection is something that very few people do.

Seriously, when was the last time you took one hour without a cell phone, or without listening to the radio or other people or watching TV?

How often do you intentionally focus on peace, quiet... instead of busily thinking about all the stuff on your to-do list?

This mile marker is about chilling out and hearing Jesus, as you reflect on what you just experienced with God and someone else.

Psalm 46:10 *"Be still and know that I am God."*

That is what Mile Marker 6 is all about.

In stillness and silence, you will hear God speak grace to your soul.

For example, one time Bruce was out fishing with his dog. After a nice time on the water, his dog had to pee. Bruce pulled his heavy boat onto a sandy beach to let the dog out to do its business.
A little while longer it was time to get back to fishing, but now there was a big wet Labrador jumping in and out of the boat. Plus, the boat was stuck on the sand.

Bruce grabbed a large rock and put it next to the boat in the shallow water. He jumped in the bow, grabbed an oar, and started to push as hard as he could against the rock to get the boat back out into deeper water.

As the dog finally got in the boat and settled down, the rock shifted, **and so did Bruce.**

Into the water he went, upside down.

He landed with the small of his back on top of the rock. He was frustrated, wounded, and soaked. Amidst some colorful language, Bruce pushed the boat out by hand and began to driving back out into open water.

Suddenly,

unexpectedly,

God spoke to him in the silence and aloneness of the moment.

Once again, this was not out loud, but in his spirit, Bruce heard God say, "Today, I just re-baptized you."

That simple word from God was so powerful and had such an impact on him, for the next several hours he didn't say a word.

He just prayed, and listened, and God continued to minister to him.

Maybe this helps you understand Mile Marker 6.

Though we all go through the hard, painful process of sharing character flaws with someone, it opens up the opportunity for God to speak to us and prepare us for removing these imperfections.

Just like a painful fall into the water, when you go through the painful experience of Mile Marker 5, you come out on the other side able to hear from God.

Jesus consistently practiced silence and solitude so He could hear from God.

Luke 5:16 *But Jesus often withdrew to lonely places and prayed.*

See, Jesus gives us a template for Mile Marker 6!

Simply go out into nature alone.

Pray,
reflect,
listen,
and prepare yourself for what God is about to do next in your life.

<table>
<tr><td>GOD SPEAKS IF WE WILL GET ALONE AND LISTEN!</td><td>It was on a run alone with God when Jesus spoke grace over Eric's life in a powerful way.

He was out in nature, praying and listening to God. Suddenly God just began to talk to him in a way he had never heard Him before.</td></tr>
</table>

The specifics of that day are personal, but what Eric experienced that day is - GOD SPEAKS IF WE WILL GET ALONE AND LISTEN!

So, now go and do it!

Take a few hours and walk, run, sit by a river. Sit by a window. But get alone.

Be outside if you can.

Turn everything off and talk to God. Then listen for Him to respond to you.
He will speak if you will listen.

Then write down what God says! We have provided space for you to journal what you heard God say to you.

_____

_____

_____

_____

_____

_____

_____

_____

_____

_____

_____

Chapter 13
Finished at The Cross

Mile Marker 7:
We believe that because of the cross
and His grace, Jesus has forgiven us
and freed us from our shortcomings.

"The cross is God's way of taking away all of our
accusations, excuses, and arguments."

- Rob Bell

Once you are to Mile Marker 7, you'll find yourself starting to experience the freedom of recovery.

You are no longer quite as tied to your addiction as you were before. Jesus and His grace have done the work to set you on the path to freedom.

Now He wants you to know that He is never going to bring up your past again.

You are **forgiven** and **freed** from your sins and shortcomings.

Psalms 103:12 *...as far as the east is from the west, so far has he removed our transgressions from us.*

Just like the east and west can never meet, you and your sins will NEVER meet again. God will NEVER bring them up!

You're
forever
forgiven,
cleared,
righteous,
and clean.

God cannot be mad at you, because your sin is no longer on you!

Isaiah 38:17 ...*in love you have delivered my life from the pit of destruction, for you have cast all my sins behind your back.* (ESV)

The Hebrew in this verse actually refers to the center of the back between the shoulder blades. It refers to that spot that you can never reach when you have an itch.

God took your sins and placed them behind His back.

He put your sins in a place **HE CAN NEVER REACH!**

He will never bring your sins back up to you - EVER! You are totally forgiven!

Micah 7:19 ...*you will tread our sins underfoot and hurl all our iniquities into the depths of the sea.*

> **Your sins are behind His back, in the depths of the sea.**

In Hebrew slang, that phrase "the depths of the sea" is a reference to a place no one can go!

When He says your sins are in the depths of the sea, they are in a place no one can go and bring them back to remind you of them!

THEY ARE GONE **FOREVER!**

You are not guilty.

You are forgiven.

You are righteous.

Because of Jesus.

We want to give you one final reminder how forgiven you are. Read the following story and then answer the questions at the end of this chapter.

John 8:1-11 *At dawn he appeared again in the temple courts, where all the people gathered around him, and he sat down to teach them. The teachers of the law and the Pharisees brought in a woman caught in adultery.*

They made her stand before the group (Can you imagine the embarrassment?) *and said to Jesus, "Teacher, this woman was caught in the act of adultery. In the Law Moses commanded us to stone such women. Now what do you say?"*

They were using this question as a trap, in order to have a basis for accusing him. But Jesus bent down and started to write on the ground with his finger.

When they kept on questioning him, he straightened up and said to them, "Let any one of you who is without sin be the first to throw a stone at her." Again he stooped down and wrote on the ground.

At this, those who heard began to go away one at a time, the older ones first, until only Jesus was left, with the woman still standing there.

Jesus straightened up and asked her, "Woman, where are they? Has no one condemned you?"

"No one, sir," she said.

"Then neither do I condemn you," Jesus declared. "Go now and leave your life of sin."

This woman was CAUGHT IN THE ACT! So, Jesus knew her sin. Yet, how did He respond to it?

_____

_____

_____

Jesus knows your sin. He caught you in the act as well. According to this story, how does He respond to you?

153

_____

_____

_____

Put yourself in this woman's situation. Do you think she wanted to go back to her life of sin, or do you think Jesus' grace empowered her to make a life change?

_____

_____

_____

God's grace says you are forgiven.

God's grace empowers you to leave your life of sin and move to something better. Write out a prayer to God and thank Him that your sins are forgiven, and you have the power to move to a better life.

_____

_____

_____

_____

_____

_____

_____

_____

Religious people always want to point out others' sins and mistakes, yet Jesus doesn't seem to act this way.

Think about your life. Are you giving others the grace He gives you? What change(s) do you need to make?

_____

_____

_____

_____

_____

_____

_____

_____

_____

_____

Now take your answers, and share them with your sponsor, mentor, or pastor.

You have made it through the rapids! WELL DONE!

You are ready to move on to Mile Marker 8.

Chapter 14
Willing to Seek Forgiveness

Mile Marker 8:
Because of God's grace toward us, we became
willing to seek forgiveness and restitution
toward all the people we have hurt.

"Mistakes are always forgivable,
if one has the courage to admit them."

- Bruce Lee

When Eric was eight, he went fishing one afternoon with his Uncle Art. Uncle Art had promised to teach him how to bass fish, and Eric was super excited.

On the way to the lake, they stopped at a bait shop. Uncle Art told him he could get one lure to use that day.

Eric had just watched a fishing show that had talked about how crankbaits with treble hooks were the thing to catch big bass. So, he begged his uncle to buy him one of those baits.

Uncle Art tried to talk him out of it, but little Eric really wanted this lure with two treble hooks. Art caved and bought it for him.

Later on that day at the lake, Eric decided to test out his new lure with all these great hooks. He reared back to cast as far as he could, but he forgot his uncle was right behind him.

He hooked his uncle right in the face with both sets of treble hooks!

This sounds bad enough, but **it gets even worse.**

The thing was, Eric didn't know that he had hooked his uncle, so he just kept jerking on the pole trying to cast while Uncle Art screamed every swear word from the history of the world!

IT WAS AWFUL!

His uncle had been kind enough to take him fishing and kind enough to buy him a new lure,
and he hooked him with it

right

in

the

face!

This story is what Mile Marker 8 is all about.

It is about writing down a list of people we know we have wronged. If Eric was making a Mile Marker 8 list, Uncle Art would definitely be on that list.

Now that God has freed you from your vice, addiction, or bad habit, it's time to think about all the people that were hurt as a result of the choices you made.

Make a list of them and become open to asking for forgiveness and making restitution for the ways you hurt them.

We found a man in Scripture that we can look to for an example. His name was Zacchaeus.

Now, Zacchaeus was **a thug.**

He made his living by shaking people down at the point of a sword, because he was tax collector.

In those days, tax collectors were the **baddest of the bad.**

They would stop at your house and say, "Pay your taxes," (always charging way more than the actual tax, so they could pocket the rest of the money for themselves). If you argued with them, they would say, "Pay what I tell you to pay, or these two Roman soldiers that are with me will break your legs, rape your wife, or burn your house down."

Of course, they always got paid.

Meet Zacchaeus - a nasty thug.

Until the day he met Jesus.

The story goes like this.

Luke 19:2-8 ...there was a man named Zacchaeus who was a chief tax collector, and he was rich. And he sought to see who Jesus was, but could not because of the crowd, for he was of short stature.

So he ran ahead and climbed up into a sycamore tree to see Him, for He was going to pass that way. And when Jesus came to the place, He looked up and saw him, and said to him, "Zacchaeus, make haste and come down, for today I must stay at your house."

So he made haste and came down, and received Him joyfully. Then Zacchaeus stood and said to the Lord, "Look, Lord, I give half of my goods to the poor; and if I have taken anything from anyone by false accusation, I restore fourfold." (NKJV)

Wow! Did you see that?

When Jesus met Zacchaeus, He never condemned him. He never beat him down for his bad behavior. Instead, He just said, "Today I want to hang out with you!"

These are Jesus' words to you also!

He doesn't want to condemn you or beat you down. He just wants to do life with you and be in relationship with you!

Jesus just wants to give you **GRACE!**

Now what is interesting is once Zach accepts Jesus' grace, he instinctively responds with what we do as we pass Mile Marker 8!

161

Luke 19:8 "Look, Lord, I give half of my goods to the poor; and if I have taken anything from anyone by false accusation, I restore fourfold." (NKJV)

Zacchaeus became willing to seek forgiveness and pay back all the people he had hurt as a tax collector!

This is what we are called to as well.

Once we experience Christ and His **life-altering** love and grace, we naturally want to go back and seek forgiveness from all the people we have hurt.

> **Once we experience Christ and His life-altering love and grace, we naturally want to go back and seek forgiveness from all the people we have hurt.**

So let's be practical.

Here is how you pass this marker:

1. Write out a list below of every person you know you hurt or wronged due to your vice, addiction, or bad habit. Then, next to each name, write down a word to describe how you hurt them. Use additional paper if needed.

_____	_____
_____	_____
_____	_____
_____	_____
_____	_____
_____	_____
_____	_____
_____	_____

2. Pray and ask Jesus to **make you willing** to ask for forgiveness from each person whose name is on your list.

Philippians 2:13 *For God is working in you, giving you the desire and the power to do what pleases him. (NLT)*

3. Ask God for the wisdom to know who on your list is someone you need to meet with - in person - to ask for their forgiveness and to make things right. Put a star by their name(s).

4. Ask God for the supernatural courage to follow through with what He told you.

Now you are ready to pass Mile Marker 9!

Chapter 15
Making it Right

Mile Marker 9:
Because of God's grace, we courageously
asked forgiveness from and made restitution
to each person we have hurt, except where to
do so would cause more harm than good.

"A man must be big enough to admit his mistakes,
smart enough to profit from them,
and strong enough to correct them."
- John C. Maxwell

Okay, now we are ready to go to the people we have hurt to confess, repent of our wrongs, and seek forgiveness and restitution from them.

Jesus gives us a great verse that we use as a motivator and wisdom for this mile marker.

Matthew 5:23-24 *Therefore, if you are offering your gift at the altar and there remember that your brother or sister has something against you, leave your gift there in front of the altar. First go and be reconciled to them; then come and offer your gift.*

Jesus is saying that He doesn't even want us to go to church if we know we have hurt someone and we haven't sought to reconcile it.

**Christ is more concerned
with relationships
than with worship services.**

We understand that this mile marker is difficult, and many people want to skip this on their way to full recovery - but you can't!

Stop and think for a second.

We hurt a lot of people with our vices, addictions, and bad habits. We can't ignore what happened; we have to deal with what happened!

We must seek to make this right to the best of our ability. **Our old way** of dealing with it was to
deny,
make excuses,
lie,
or use the easy out, saying, "Oops! I'm sorry!"

Now that we have found Christ and experienced His grace, we recognize that we must actually seek forgiveness and restitution! This also helps those we've hurt, so they can find freedom as well.

> **Now is time to make things right.**
>
> **It doesn't have to be scary.**
>
> **Remember, you have the Spirit of God in you now!**

Now is time to make things right.

It doesn't have to be scary.

Remember, you have the Spirit of God in you now!

One time Bruce went to make things right with one of his drinking buddies. He had been sober for close to a year and hadn't seen or heard from this guy.

Bruce tried calling to set up an appointment, but there was no answer. One day he decided to just drive over to this man's house and knock on the door.

The door opened up and there was his old buddy greeting him at the door.

With a shotgun in his hands.

Freaked out… yeah, Bruce definitely knows what that feels like.

Bruce told him that he wanted to make things right, and that he was hoping to be forgiven for harming his old friend. His buddy, not being in a healthy place, told him to get off his property and never show his face again.

Bruce did what any rational, quick-witted, nimble guy would do.

He ran.

FAST.

This might sound like a scary situation, and frankly, it was. Thankfully, the Holy Spirit was with Bruce protecting him. But Bruce has peace now because he was able to ask for forgiveness.

He had "swept his side of the street."

Back in his drinking days, one night Bruce shot a bow and arrow through a telephone pole conduit and knocked out all of the power in his hometown - thirty thousand homes!

Now, that's pretty crazy.

But here's the really funny (we mean, bad) part: It was the night of the big Mike Tyson vs. Evander Holyfield boxing match. You know the fight, Tyson ate Holyfield's ear!

People had spent $40.00 to watch the fight on pay-per-view.

Due to the power outage, all those who had ordered the fight lost the programming they had paid for and had to reorder it once the power came back on.

Once Bruce got to this part of his recovery journey, he realized that there wasn't anything that he could do to reconcile the financial loss with the city or anyone who'd ordered the fight.

He went to the city offices and told them that he needed to help make right what he wronged in his drinking days. He asked for forgiveness. The city agreed to allow him to serve one hundred hours of community service.

So in 1999, on the northern suburban streets of St. Paul, Bruce walked along every ditch and picked up trash and debris until he completed his one hundred hours.

169

He's not the only one who made amends. Mike Tyson gave Evander Holyfield his ear back, too. Remember that old Foot Locker commercial? He said he kept it in formaldehyde.

These are just a couple of examples of what one person in recovery did to make right what he wronged.

What if you went back to some of the people you wronged and made things right?

You'll find yourself freed from all those little hooks that are still hanging on as a result of those circumstances.

You will understand another depth of God's grace.

When you are ready to take action, here are suggestions to guide you:

1. Make an appointment with each person you hurt.

Call them on the phone, email them, or have someone take a message to them for you.

Say something like, "I know I have hurt you in a deep and personal way, and I want to make it right. God has really been working on me, and I know I wronged you. I would like to meet you in person. Is it possible for us to meet? Please let me seek to learn how I can make things right with you."

If they say yes, ask them when they're available and make arrangements to meet them at a destination of their choice. Ideally, it's nice to meet somewhere neutral like a coffee shop or restaurant.

If they refuse to meet with you, consult your sponsor, pastor, or priest and ask them for permission to write this person a letter. (This is a letter for your own release, they will never see it; but you will submit it to God and move forward free.)

2. A word of caution.

We suggest you don't go back to an old flame when they're married or in a new relationship. That's only going to hurt the spouse or significant other and, more than likely, tick them off. If you need to make things right with them, write them a letter. Ask Jesus to help that person find forgiveness in their heart for your wrongs. Take a walk, pray for them, and burn the letter.

Also, if you were involved in sexual violence, assault, or other crime-related matters, you need to seek out a professional counselor, pastor, or priest before going to those you have victimized.

Seek out their guidance about how to approach the situation. Be willing to turn yourself in to the authorities if there are criminal charges pending.

3. When you meet with the people you wronged, tell them which part you played in the wrongdoing.

Try not to get hung up in the details of the story and prove how they were wrong too. Don't address how you may have been right. Just tell them that what you did was not right and ask if there's anything you can do to make it better.

Once they've told you how you can make it right, honor their request to the best of your ability.

4. Here is a suggested template of what to say when you have a forgiveness conversation:

"Thank you for meeting with me today. I know that in the past I was wrong. I don't expect us to have a new relationship, I just know that I hurt you in the past. I was so wrong, would you please forgive me? Would you be willing to tell me what I can do to make things right with you?"

From here, just listen to how they respond. Let them respond however they choose. Thank them again for meeting with you, honor their requests, and humbly walk away knowing that you did the best you could to retify the memory of your relationship.

5. Be realistic!

Some people will tell you to jump off a bridge and get the heck out of their lives. Honor them by leaving them alone, but don't go jump off a bridge. Remember, they are hurt, and it is okay for them to feel how they feel.

You just do what you know is the right thing by seeking forgiveness.

We like to call this "cleaning up our side of the street".

We can't clean up our neighbor's yard, but we can clean up our yard. That is what our responsibility is - to come clean about our part and seek forgiveness and reconciliation to the best of our ability.

6. Sometimes people will not want to reconcile; they will want to fight.

Do not fight them! Just leave them alone.

You have done all you can do. Move on with your life.

Don't let them draw you into their world of bitterness and despair! Their resentment does not have to suck you in!

7. Sometimes there is healing, and a relationship can be beautifully restored.

This is the amazing thing about this mile marker - God uses it to bring healing.

8. Tell your pastor, priest, mentor, or sponsor that you talked to each and every person on your list.

Let them celebrate your freedom with you!

Now you are ready to move onto Mile Marker 10!

Chapter 16
Living By His Grace

Mile Marker 10:
We live life in Christ "by His grace."
Therefore, when we are wrong,
we promptly admit it to God and others.

"I know for me, going back the person I've
bad-mouthed or lied to is absolutely humiliating!
But isn't it interesting that "humiliating"
has the same root word as "humility"?
Part of humility is taking responsibility for my sin and
asking forgiveness, even when it doesn't feel good.
God wants to heal and restore
your relationships, but it's not easy."

- Chip Ingram

.

Once you've reached this mile marker, we want you to know you that you are in a really good spot. Just like when you finally get to a good fishing spot, you have reached a place where you can start to see some results of all your hard work.

God's grace has lead you on a journey that has landed you with a **new life** and a **new start!**

Everything up to this point has been about you working on yourself and allowing grace to work with you.

This mile marker is all about maintaining this new way of life and building better relationships with others.

Fishing is always fun with a couple of buddies.

Whenever you get a couple of fishermen in a boat, a competition starts to happen. It doesn't take long until we're keeping track of how many fish we have caught and how few fish the other guy has caught.

If you don't fish, let us tell you that this is when fishing starts to get really competitive! There is a pride that comes out in us when we can pick on the other guy for not catching anything. Pride comes out when we catch a huge fish or catch a ton of them and the other guys don't do as well.

Out of balance, this pride can lead us to brag, look down on others, and sometimes even put others down. By the end of the day, we can really make other people feel bad. If the other guys didn't do as well, we can make them feel foolish.

This pride thing damages our friendships, our personal reputation, and our ability to truly enjoy our lives.

That is why we must take Mile Marker 10 seriously. It is all about maintaining an attitude of humility.

Just because we have found some sobriety doesn't mean we are superior to others. What got us into our addiction in the first place was the sin of "doing our own thing" and thinking we could avoid the consequences.

That is just plain ol' pride.

To avoid a relapse we must stay humble!

Proverbs 13:10 Where there is strife, there is pride, but wisdom is found in those who take advice.

Prideful people don't ask for help.

People of wisdom and humility ask for suggestions from other people.

They honor and respect others.

They are always seeking to learn new techniques for staying in the flow of grace, just like a fisherman asks another fisherman what kind of bait is working right now.

Pride causes strife and division.

Humility brings unity and allows relationships to prosper.

Proverbs 11:2 When pride comes, then comes disgrace, but with humility comes wisdom.

We want you to notice that there is a difference between being humiliated and being humble. When you are able to promptly admit when you're wrong and ask others for advice, you are living out humility.

176

When you are living in humility, it is really hard to end up humiliated.

On the other hand, if you will not admit your mistakes and they are found out (and they always are), eventually you will be humiliated.

This is much more painful than just owning up to your mistakes.

Jesus speaks of humility this way, and if anyone would know how to live a humble life, it would be Him, right?

Matthew 23:12 And whoever exalts himself will be humbled, and he who humbles himself will be exalted. (NKJV)

In other words, the person that tries to be better than everyone else will end up humbled, but the person that maintains an attitude of humility will eventually be given a place to influence others for good.

Now we need to make one thing clear: humility is not putting yourself down or being negative about yourself.

You can catch more fish than other people.

You can do well in life.

> **Pride is pointing to your success, humility is pointing to Jesus' grace toward you.**

Just don't make others feel bad about it.

Pride is pointing to your success, humility is pointing to Jesus' grace toward you.
You are where you are in life because Jesus is good to you, not because you have figured out how to succeed on your own.

It is all because of His **RIVER OF GRACE!**

So, as you're starting to pass this mile marker, we want to give you a couple of questions to ask yourself daily:

1. Where was I wrong today?

_____

_____

_____

_____

2. Who do I need to go to tomorrow to make it right?

_____

_____

_____

_____

3. What do I need to do tomorrow to make it right?

_____

_____

_____

_____

4. Did pride get in the way of my recovery or faith today?

_____

_____

_____

_____

5. What did I do well today?

_____

_____

_____

_____

It's good practice to answer these questions daily and realize what you need to make right. Promptly make it right with God and the people you wronged.

Once you're able to get to the end of the day and honestly say that you didn't really hurt anyone, you will see how your faith is growing.

It is so cool to see how much progress you've made, and turn it into gratitude to God.

Now you're ready to experience Mile Marker 11!

Chapter 17
Daily Connection to Grace

Mile Marker 11:
We seek through daily prayer and the Word of God to better understand the depths of God's grace for us and His will for our lives.

"If a drunk comes to a service... (Christians say) 'Brother, God loves you.'... But woe to that drunk if he comes back drunk after being saved. God loved him when he was a sinner and drunk, but if he's born again and he's still drunk – God forbid! Most Christians would not offer the same kind of unconditional love. Doesn't something seem inconsistent about that? Grace is not just for the lost. Christians must live by grace too."[1]

\- Andrew Wommack

Every lake has deep parts and shallow parts.

The same is true for the grace of God.

Some people live with shallow grace, which can be defined as: God gives you grace until you become a Christian. But once you are a Christian, if you mess up, you are now a lowlife loser!

Every Christian around you who messes up is a lowlife loser as well.

That is not deep, full, rich grace.

That is condemnation.

Shallow.
Natural.
Unspiritual grace.

Deep, rich, full grace looks like this:

No matter
what you do
or where you go,
no matter how you act or what you accomplish in life,

you are **ALWAYS**

deeply loved,

**highly favored,
greatly blessed,**

totally righteous,

and destined to reign

...because of Jesus.

This is the deep, rich, full grace that God wants you to come to know and understand as you read His word, pray, and live your life today.

Let's go out into the deep part of the lake for a while.

You are deeply loved.

Before the creation of the world, God loved you.

When you drew your first breath, God loved you.

When you kissed a girl, God loved you.

When you won that award, God loved you.

You know what else?

God loved you the day you made your **biggest mistake**.

God loved you just as much when you were
drunk
or high
or looking at porn
or eating too much
or gambling
or lying
or cheating
or living in sexual misconduct.

You were loved on your worst day
as much as on your best day.

> **You were loved
> on your
> worst day
> as much
> as on your
> best day.**

184

No matter what you do.
No matter what you did.
No matter what you will do.
No matter where you go.
No matter how good or bad
you think you are...

YOU ARE LOVED!

There is nothing you can do about it.
You can't escape His love.
You can't out-sin His love.
You can't stop His love.

God just deeply loves you!

Romans 8:38-39 *For I am convinced that neither death nor life, neither angels nor demons, neither the present nor the future, nor any powers, neither height nor depth, nor anything else in all creation, will be able to separate us from the love of God that is in Christ Jesus our Lord.*

You are highly favored.

Favor isn't fair.

Favor means that special advantage is given to one over the other. The moment you gave your life to Christ, you were given special advantage. You came into the family of God, and God always gives special treatment to His sons and daughters.

When you get up in the morning, know the sun is shining because God has favor for you.

When you go to work, know that God is going before you because God has favor for you.

When you drop your kids off at school, expect that God's favor is protecting and surrounding them.

When you need an idea, expect God to give you great wisdom because His favor is on you.

When you open your mail, expect to see God's favor on your finances and bills.

When you need power to avoid temptation, trust that God's hand is on you, so you have all the power you need to do the right thing.

Why?

Because you are **highly favored!**

Psalm 5:12 *Surely, LORD, you bless the righteous; you surround them with your favor as with a shield.*

You are greatly blessed.

God is the God of blessing.

Every gift you have ever received is the blessing of God on your life.

Your health is the blessing of God.

Your kids are a blessing from God.

Your wife or husband is a blessing from God.

Your house, car, and the food in your fridge is a blessing from God.

You don't just have physical blessings; you have spiritual blessings in Christ as well.

Your recovery is a blessing from God.

Your forgiveness is a blessing from God.

Your joy is a blessing from God.

Your wisdom is a blessing from God.

God blesses His children with countless blessings!
Look around and try to count them; you will be astounded! You
are **greatly blessed!**

Ephesians 1:3 *Praise be to the God and Father of our Lord
Jesus Christ, who has blessed us in the heavenly realms with
every spiritual blessing in Christ.*

You are totally righteous.

You used to suck.

You were a sinner.

You made lots of mistakes.

You were dis-approved.

You were displeasing.

You were guilty.

You were hooked!

You were ashamed. **But not anymore!**

You have been washed in the blood of Jesus Christ. You have
been cleansed and cleared of all sin. You have been healed and
restored into a full and beautiful relationship with the Heavenly
Father.

You have been given credit for Christ's righteousness.

You have been approved. You have been sanctified.

Justified.

"Just as if I'd never sinned."

"Just as if I'd always obeyed."

You are justified.

This is how God sees you now.

You used to be a sinner, but now you are a saint.

It is **WHO YOU ARE**, because of **WHOSE YOU ARE!**

There is nothing you can do about it.

You didn't earn it.

You didn't accomplish it.

You can't lose it.

You can't sin your way out of it.

Your sins are atoned for.

Your life has been made new.

You have been set free.

This gift of righteousness is irrevocable.

You are **totally righteous!**

2 Corinthians 5:21 God made him who knew no sin to be sin for us so that in him we might become the righteousness of God.

You are destined to reign.

Before Christ,
sin reigned over you,
addiction reigned over you,
fear controlled you,
depression destroyed you,
vices lured you,
Satan and his servants devoured you.

You were like a fish on a line, destined to be caught and killed.

THIS IS NOT THE CASE ANY LONGER!

You gave your **life** to Christ.

You gave your **body** to Christ.

You gave your **soul** to Christ.

When this happened, the power of sin over you was cut.

You went from
powerless to powerful.

You went from
dominated to dominating.

You went from
the prison to the palace.

You went from
struggling to strength.

You went from
victim to victor!

You are not a pauper anymore.

You are a prince or princess of God Most High, and you rule
and reign with Christ!

You are **destined to reign!**

Romans 5:17 *For if, by the trespass of the one man, death
reigned through that one man, how much more will those who
receive God's abundant provision of grace and of the gift of
righteousness reign in life through the one man, Jesus Christ!*

This is WHO YOU ARE because of Jesus and His grace.

When you believe every day that you are deeply loved, highly
favored, greatly blessed, totally righteous, and destined to
reign because of Jesus, you wake up every day at peace.

You wake up secure in life.

You wake up without stress or worry.

You are content and safe, knowing God is taking good care of you and has a great plan for you!

You wake up knowing God already conquered your addiction at the cross, and you are already free.

You cannot be a slave because of Jesus and His grace.

**WELCOME TO
DEEP,
FULL,
RICH,
SUPERNATURAL GRACE!**

What if you believed this for yourself?

Wouldn't it be awesome to wake up every day believing that about yourself? How could you get up and remind yourself of the depths of God's grace for you every day?

That is what Mile Marker 11 is really all about.

We suggest every day that you get up and seek to hear God's grace spoken over you by practicing 3 simple things:

1. Start your day with prayer.

As soon as you get up, hit your knees before your feet. Ask God to talk to you. Thank Him for His love. Invite Him to lead you and guide you that day.

Practice inviting God into your day as soon as you get up. This will help you be aware of God all day long.

2. Read your Bible before you do anything else.

The Bible is full of practical wisdom that will help you grow in your faith and maintain a healthy lifestyle. Read a little bit every day and try journaling, too.

Spending even a few minutes with God daily will set you up for success in life. You can practice the SOAP method:

Scripture - What was the verse or phrase that stuck out to you most today?

Observation - What does that verse or phrase mean to you?

Application - What is God telling you to do as a result of reading this verse or phrase today?

Prayer - Write out a prayer to God based on what He told you.

Try this! Studying the Bible keeps God's words alive in you!

3. End your day with a prayer of forgiveness and gratitude.

Before you go to sleep, give God your regrets from the day. Tell Him you are sorry for the wrong you did and ask Him for the power to seek forgiveness from those you may have hurt.

Thank God for His blessings that day!

Every day you can thank God for
a person that loves you,
a possession that brings you joy,
a past experience that made you happy,
or a new possibility that God brought your way.

Do this daily and you will live a happier, healthier life.

[1]WOMMACK, ANDREW; THE TRUE NATURE OF GOD, p.78
Andrew Wommack Ministries - 2011

Chapter 18
Sharing His Grace

Mile Marker 12:
Having been set free by the grace of God, we seek
to bring freedom and grace to others as well.

"I serve a higher power, Jesus Christ.
I make no apologies in saying that."

- Rick Warren

When you've reached Mile Marker 12, you know you're at a place of completion. You have arrived in a sweet spot of God's destiny for you!

Congratulations on getting to this incredible place in your life. When you first started out on this journey of recovery, it seemed so far down the river that you'd never get there!

But you made it!

God did not fail you!

Now we have good news for you:

THIS IS NOT THE END OF YOUR JOURNEY!

This is just the place where God now says to you, "Now you are ready. I can use you. I have a plan for you. I unhooked you so you could help others get unhooked!"

Here's how Jesus talked about this mile marker:

Matthew 4:19 *"Follow me and I will make you fishers of men."*

John 20:21 *"As the Father has sent me, so I am sending you."*

Think of it like a fishing trip.

When you arrive at your destination, the journey is not over - it is just beginning! Now you get to experience the joy of catching fish!

That's Mile Marker 12. The other eleven mile markers were the journey; Mile Marker 12 is the experience of catching fish!

We need to make an important statement here:

**You might be experiencing your destiny,
but you're still connected to your history.**

Just like an old fisherman tells stories to the younger guys about places he has been and fish he has caught, when you get to Mile Marker 12, you have success stories and life experience that others need to hear about and learn from.

You know your story better than anyone else. You are the one who lived it!

It's not about all the problems that led up to launching into the flow of grace, but the solutions that you found along the way. The solutions to those problems are now your history.

Now you get the opportunity to share with others how great an experience you have had. You have a success story that others need to hear, **especially those who are still on their journey.**

Your experience of grace and the life of freedom is a story every addict can draw power and inspiration from.

They will think, "If that guy/girl can make it -- if God changed them -- He can change me!"

> **You are a guide to someone else's freedom!**

Your story can inspire someone to stay sober or clean for 24 more hours.

You are a guide to someone else's freedom!

196

You might be wondering, "How do I share my experience of God's grace with someone else?"

Let's talk about fishing again.

One of our favorite times of the fishing season is when we get to bring a beginner with us in the boat. We get to show them all the different lure choices and explain why we have so many different types of rods and reels.

We'll show them the hot spots and teach them how to cast a lure right up into the tight spot where we know a big fish lies.

But before we even get out on the water, we always equip ourselves with the necessities so we have everything we need to be successful.

This is what we must do in recovery.

We need to equip ourselves with the right stuff so we can be successful at fishing for people.

Here's the equipment you need:

1. Arm yourself in the Word of God.

Read the Bible daily.

Know it.

Learn it.

Hebrews 4:12 For the word of God is living and active. Sharper than any double-edged sword, it penetrates even to dividing soul and spirit...

2 Timothy 4:2 Preach the word! Be ready in season and out of season... (NKJV)

You never know when you might run into someone who needs the good news of Jesus. You want to know the Bible so you can help others understand it.

2. Pray, pray, pray.

Pray that you have the opportunity to reach someone who doesn't know Jesus.

Pray for His peace to surround you as you share your mile markers and faith with someone else. Pray for spiritual protection from enemy attacks.

Here's a quick story about the power of prayer:

Acts 16:25-26 *Around midnight Paul and Silas were praying and singing hymns to God, and the other prisoners were listening. Suddenly, there was a massive earthquake, and the prison was shaken to its foundations. All the doors immediately flew open, and the chains of every prisoner fell off! (NLT)*

Prayer shook the foundations, broke open doors, and shattered chains.

Ask God to do that in your friends' lives.

Ask Him to shake their foundations, open up doors for you to speak to them, and shatter the chains of their addictions as well.

God loves to answer prayers like this!

3. Open your mouth and actually talk with someone.

Isaiah 6:8 *Then I heard the voice of the Lord saying, "Whom shall I send? And who will go for us?" And I said, "Here I am, send me!"*

God's heart is that His lost kids find healing and help. He wants to send someone, so open up your mouth and say, "I will go!"

198

Sharing what grace and recovery has done for you requires you to actually open up and say something to people. You never know what people need if you never ask them.

You just might find that you thrive at this, but you won't know until you start to talk to others.

4. Go for the ask.

When you talk to people about Jesus, ask them if they'd like to have a relationship with Christ, too.

Say something like: "So, would you like to pray and ask Jesus to forgive your past and lead your future?"

Lead them in a prayer to trust Christ as their Forgiver and Leader.

5. Ask God to reveal the calling He has placed over your life.

God does this work in you so that He can work through you!

God has something specific He wants you to do now that He has set you free from your vice, addiction, or bad habit.

Ask Him to reveal it to you.

Ephesians 2:10 *For we are God's masterpiece. He has created us anew in Christ Jesus, so we can do the good things he planned for us long ago. (NLT)*

6. Invite your friends and family to church and your recovery meeting.

Many times, people find freedom and stay free as they meet together with other people of faith and recovery.

It is these meetings that keep people growing and committed to continuing on down the river of grace.

Hebrews 10:25 Let us not give up meeting together, as some are in the habit of doing, but encourage one another... (NLT)

Eric and Bruce both truly love Mile Marker 12.

Our greatest joy in life is not catching the biggest fish.

It is seeing
a broken,
hurting life
find God's grace
and be set free
from whatever
had them hooked.

Eric's motivation for preaching every weekend at church is that one more lost, broken, and hurting soul will cross the line of faith and find the grace of God.

Bruce leads two recovery meetings each week. He shares his personal experiences with the mile markers and tells the stories of what happened along the way.

We want to end this chapter by sharing with you Christ's heart for lost and broken people one more time.

We hope these verses help you catch a vision for how God wants to use you to help others find freedom.

Revelation 22:14-17 Blessed are those who wash their robes (Christians), that they may have the right to the tree of life and may go through the gates into the city (heaven).

Outside are the dogs (addicts, sinners, and broken people), those who practice magic arts (drug dealers and users), the sexually immoral (porn addicts), the murderers, the idolaters and everyone who loves and practices a good lie (addicts).

The Spirit and the bride (Jesus and the church) say, "Come!"

And let him who hears say, "Come!"

200

Whoever is thirsty, let him come;

and whoever wishes, let him take the free gift of the water of life.

Notice Jesus' words to those outside who are broken and messed up is **not condemnation**, it is COME!

Let all who are thirsty COME!

Jesus wants to use you as His mouthpiece.

He wants you to say, "COME!"

It doesn't matter who you are, who you sleep with, or how many drugs you have done, you are welcome in the house of God.

You are welcome with the people of God.

You are welcome to ask Jesus to forgive you and lead you and take you down the river of His grace!

We who have found freedom have the joy of shouting every day to everyone, "COME! Jesus has the answers! HIS GRACE IS ENOUGH!"

Now that God has changed your life, go and change your world!

Congratulations!

You have journeyed down the river of grace!

Your future awaits you!

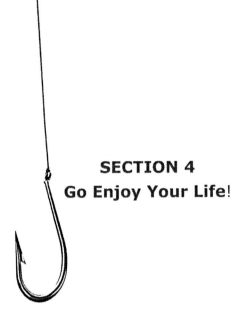

SECTION 4
Go Enjoy Your Life!

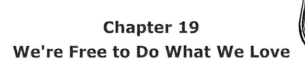

Chapter 19
We're Free to Do What We Love

"I like to get high on something,
and when I asked the Lord to come and make his
home inside of me, the spiritual high, it's so real.
And I hate religion - I don't talk about religion at all -
but the relationship through Christ is what I found.
And I'm totally satisfied...
Now I can enjoy anything I do. It's the best high ever."

- Brian "Head" Welch[1]

We wrap up this book with a few thoughts about living the good life.

Once you are freed from your addiction, vice, or bad habit, **you are free to go have a life!**

Think about that! Before you were held back, snagged by your struggle.

Now, you are free to go
succeed at a business,
have a great marriage,
take trips to far off places,
and meet interesting people.

Just like a fish gets to swim off to its destiny when it throws the hook, you and I get to go after a "rich and satisfying life." (John 10:10)

This is true for both Bruce and Eric. We want to share with you a few of our "sober" stories, in hopes it will inspire you to keep moving forward in faith.

Since Bruce has been addiction-free, he has had the time to enjoy musky fishing.

Last year, Bruce was fishing on his favorite lake, using live bait that was 16-18 inches long. In the course of five days, he and his friend caught 18 muskies, the smallest of which was 40 inches. There were multiple fish that were more than 48 inches long!

Another time, Bruce took his elderly father Bruce Sr., and daughter Rita out on the lake. They were using the same technique that had brought Bruce his previous success. He recalled that about a week earlier he had seen a gigantic fish follow in, but he couldn't get it to bite.

He and his family decided to go after it.

In less than twenty minutes, they had caught his attention, and the big fish ate!

Bruce had the dilemma of deciding whether to reel it in himself, or to let Bruce Sr. or Rita have the honor. As the fish held onto the bait, Bruce handed the rod over to Rita, who ended up reeling in the biggest fish to ever enter Bruce's boat!

A whopping 53 inches with a 27-inch girth (that's the measurement around the belly). That musky ended up weighing 49.73 pounds, and is currently unhooked and loving life in Bruce's secret lake.

This experience would not have been nearly as awesome if Bruce was still tied to his addiction. Sobriety makes the good days so much more satisfying. It also makes the bad days easier to endure.

Life is just better now that we are unhooked and untangled from what used to hold us captive.

Eric, too, now has a much different life since he became free of his workaholism and approval addiction. He now rarely works more than 40 hours a week. He takes one day off each week. His family enjoys vacations every year. He's been to almost every state in the U.S. with his wife and kids. They are planning a trip to Israel later this year.

Doing life with his family is so much better than living for work or for the approval of others!

Eric fishes almost every week in the summer now, too.

Getting to do the things he loves with the people he loves, having a life, and not caring what others think has truly brought happiness and stability to his soul.

His stress level is down,
his joy is up,
and his ability to hear from God is much greater.

These are some happy, hook-free stories we have because Jesus Christ has freed us.

What stories do you want to tell?

With your newfound freedom, you can dream again.

You can have goals again.

You can go and do whatever you want to do!

So, what do you want to do with the rest of your life?

Psalm 37:4 *Take delight in the LORD, and he will give you your heart's desires. (NLT)*

If you follow God and stay close to Him, He will put a dream in your heart and help you live it out!

So, what is it? What are your heart's desires? What stories do you want to tell five years from now?

Take a few minutes and write down the dreams you have for the rest of your life:

_____

_____

_____

_____

_____

_____

> **Grace has done for us what nothing else could: it has made life worth living.**

Grace has done for us what nothing else could: it has made life worth living.

So, go for it!

If you love downhill skiing, go plan out a great trip and fly down a black diamond.

If you want go overseas on a great vacation, make plans now to do it!

If you want to start a business -- do it!

You can't enjoy life until you start to enjoy life!

The world is open to you!

You're free to thrive!

That's what your good God wants for you.

That's what we want for you, too.

[1]http://www.blabbermouth.net/news/korns-brian-head-welch-says-he-hates-religion-has-found-satisfaction-in-relationship-through-christ/#I47db2uQao0wDxk5.99

Chapter 20
We're Free to Be Who We Want to Be

"Be yourself, because everyone else is taken."
- Tommy Lee

Now this is the good part...

Like a big fish swimming away from the boat and waving goodbye with its tail, being set free means a new lease on life!

It means we can finally breathe again and wave (our tails) goodbye to what had us hooked.

Wave yo' ass at yo' past!

Or, in other words, wave yo' ass at yo' past.

Bruce often says that on a scale of 1-10, his life is a 13. This is the freedom mindset that Jesus wants for each of us! He wants us to experience all the richness and fullness and freedom of life that He planned out when He created us.

Psalm 23:5-6 *You prepare a feast for me in the presence of my enemies. You honor me by anointing my head with oil. My cup overflows with blessings. Surely your goodness and unfailing love will pursue me all the days of my life, and I will live in the house of the LORD forever. (NLT)*

You used to have this enemy called addiction, but Christ has prepared a table for you in the presence of your enemy! Now you cup overflows with blessing.

God wants His kids to have a full and satisfying life!

He is not against you marrying that person or buying that new house. He is okay with you driving a decent vehicle and having a job that you love.

He wants these good things for you!

But what He wants most is for you to be happy, free, and full of joy and hope.

His desire is that you would have an overflowing cup of life!

Tim McGraw sings a song about a dad who inspires his son to live a full life; to live "like he was dying." He said he went "sky-diving", "Rocky Mountain climbing", and went "2.7 seconds on a bull named Fu Manchu."

This good father wants his son to not let life pass him by. This is what your Father in Heaven hopes and dreams for your life as well!

We understand that you may have thought God is about rules and a list of do-and-don'ts, but this is not the Jesus we know.

We know a Jesus that wants more for you than religious piety.

This is the God we know:

1 Timothy 6:17 *...God, who richly provides us with everything for our enjoyment.*

You don't have to wait to enjoy your life until you've died and gone to heaven. God wants you to enjoy Him and all He has for you *now*!

So, do it. Be who God created you to be!

Don't stress out about trying to be perfect! Just be yourself.

Worship God,
listen to God,
and love God, but be you!

Christ will lead you to a good future!

There is a passage in the Old Testament where God speaks to His people and tells them His vision for their lives. We want you to see it.

Ezekiel 36:33-36
On the day I cleanse you from all your sins,

(God did that for you at the cross.)

I will resettle your towns, and the ruins will be rebuilt. The desolate land will be cultivated instead of lying desolate in the sight of all who pass through it.

(In other words, your body is a temple that has laid desolate to the abuse it took because of addiction, but God is cultivating you again! God is rebuilding you. You are cut out to thrive!)

They will say, "This land that was laid waste has become like the garden of Eden; the cities that were lying in ruins, desolate and destroyed, are now fortified and inhabited."

(That is what God did when He freed you from your vice, addiction, or bad habit. He rebuilt you stronger, wiser, and more secure than before.)

The nations around you that remain will know that I the Lord have rebuilt what was destroyed and have replanted what was desolate. I the Lord have spoken, AND I WILL DO IT.

(People around you will notice that you are changed, restored, and whole. They will know it was God and His grace that did it, not your own strength or power.)

Galatians 5:22-25 *The fruit of the Spirit [what comes with God in control] is love, joy, peace, patience, kindness, goodness, faithfulness, gentleness and self-control. Against such things there is no law.*

This is the real
FULL and ABUNDANT LIFE!

This is who God created you to be.
He wants you full of
love,
joy,
patience,
and kindness,
**no matter what
life throws at you.**

God wants to give you the ability
to be
good,
faithful,
gentle, and
self-controlled,
even when others around you are not.

THIS IS THE NEW YOU!

It is who you were created to be. So start living it today.

James 4:14 What is your life? You are a mist that appears for a little while and then vanishes.

In other words, **life is short.** You are here only for a short while, so live while you have the chance.

> **Set yourself up to do what you love for the little time you get.**
>
> **Choose today to thrive - don't wait for tomorrow.**

Be who you want to be with the little time you have left.

Choose today to thrive. Don't wait for tomorrow. In Latin, *Carpe Diem,* "Seize the Day"! Do it... seize your day!

You don't know what tomorrow will hold -- or even if you'll have tomorrow.

Eric has a weird request for after he dies (you have to know Eric's sense of humor to fully appreciate this).
He's asked to be cremated, and then he's instructed his son, Braden, to take the ashes to a river, catch a northern or a bass, sprinkle some of the ashes down its mouth, and let it go.

Why? It's the circle of **life.**

Eric has been eating northern and bass his whole life, so when he dies, the fish gets to take a bite out of him! It is a morbid joke, but Eric and Braden think it's hilarious. You are going to be gone soon, so you might as well make a plan.

Soon you will be a name on a headstone. On the headstone will be your birthdate and death date. Everything you did, said, or thought will be between those two dates. Your whole life will have happened during that hyphen.

What will people say about you?

What will they say you were like?

Live the heck out of your hyphen and become the person you want to be! **Carpe Diem!**

The best way to honor God your Creator is to thrive in how He created you.

Take some time and write down a bucket list of things you want to do before you die. Write at least 15 things you want to experience before you kick the bucket.

Make it personal. Include things you want to do with your relationships and family, your work, your travel, your finances and your faith.

Personal Goals:

1. _____

2. _____

3. _____

Marriage & Family Goals:

1. _____
2. _____
3. _____

Career Goals:

1. _____
2. _____
3. _____

Financial Goals:

1. _____
2. _____
3. _____

Faith Goals:

1. _____
2. _____
3. _____

Now pray over these goals and ask God to help you accomplish each one.

Psalm 37:4 *Take delight in the L*ORD*, and he will give you the desires of your heart.*

GO LIVE LIFE UNHOOKED & UNTANGLED!

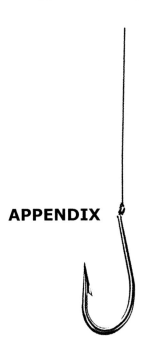

APPENDIX

Our Grace-Based Teaching Material

We examined all of our teaching material and measured it against grace. We looked at every packet or handout we've ever created.

If the material asked someone to achieve something to find freedom, it was thrown out. We moved from a position of hard work to a position of suggestion.

Any good recovery meeting out there suggests that you really look at their materials and use them to get to work.

Grace offers a beautiful flow of suggestion that allows people to find freedom. Grace is an organic recovery experience. This helps people want to consider a recovery lifestyle.

Having someone tell you that you won't measure up if you don't achieve is what brought many people to a place of needing recovery in the first place!

We came up with a new system of offering suggestions while keeping people connected to a flow of grace.

Please help yourself to any of this material.

The 12 Mile Markers

Mile Marker 1: We admit we are powerless over our vice, addiction, or bad habit, and our lives are unmanageable.

Mile Marker 2: Came to believe that Jesus and the power of His grace is the only thing that can free me and restore me to sanity.

Mile Marker 3: We turned our will and our lives over to the care of Jesus and His grace!

Mile Marker 4: We examined ourselves and the root causes that led us to our vices, addictions and bad habits.

Mile Marker 5: We admit to ourselves, another person, and Jesus the exact nature of our wrongs, and throw ourselves into Christ's mercy and grace.

Mile Marker 6: We became open for Jesus to remove our defects of character.

Mile Marker 7: We believe that because of the cross and His grace, Jesus has forgiven us and freed us from our shortcomings.

Mile Marker 8: Because of God's grace toward us, we became willing to seek forgiveness and restitution toward all the people we have hurt.

Mile Marker 9: Because of God's grace, we courageously asked forgiveness from and made restitution to each person we have hurt, except where to do so would cause more harm than good.

Mile Marker 10: We live life in Christ "by His grace." Therefore, when we are wrong, we promptly admit it to God and others.

Mile Marker 11: We seek through daily prayer and the Word of God to better understand the depths of God's grace for us and His will for our lives.

Mile Marker 12: Having been set free by the grace of God, we seek to bring freedom and grace to others as well.

About the Authors

Eric Dykstra is a former freaked-out Christian overachiever who is now resting in the grace of God found in the New Covenant. He and his wife Kelly founded The Crossing, a multi-site church north of Minneapolis. Eric's passions include seeing broken people far from God come to know the amazing grace of Jesus, fishing on the Rum River for smallmouth bass, and traveling with his family.

Bruce Rauma was caught up in bondage to drugs and alcohol for many years until Jesus set him free in November 1997. He and his wife Diane have a God-given goal to reach as many lives as possible with the grace and freedom that only Jesus Christ can offer. Together they lead the WOW Church of the Nazarene in Backus, MN, and Bruce spends his free time chasing muskies in Northern Minnesota. His favorite thing in the world is helping people who have been hooked live a life free in Christ.

Find The Crossing Church's ministry on the web:

PastorEricDykstra.com (Eric's blog)
KellyDykstra.com (Kelly's blog)
Twitter: @EricDykstra @KellyDykstra @CrossingChurch

Their sermons may be found on freegrace.tv

The Crossing (freegrace.tv) is based in Elk River, Minnesota, with campuses in surrounding towns. It is known widely for its unique approach to reaching those who feel the need for God's grace the most. The grace message and its accompanying Holy Spirit power is continually transforming the people of The Crossing.

The Crossing College (TheCrossingCollege.com) equips members of the Body of Christ to live out their calling.

Crossing Creative (CrossingCreative.com) leads The Crossing in worship and publishes original worship music. *Grace is Life* is their debut album, combining intentional, grace-centric lyrics with their signature rock & roll-style of worship. Their second album is called *Found My Worth*. Both are available on iTunes and Amazon.

If you liked this book, you might like

by Eric Dykstra

An excerpt from *Grace on Tap*

Grace is the truth, the whole truth, and nothing but the truth! We don't need to balance grace with the truth. Grace is totally imbalanced. It is crazy. It is overwhelming goodness, mercy, and favor to sinners who did nothing to deserve it, earn it, or achieve it!

Let me explain why this matters practically. If we believe we need to balance grace and truth, we end up living in bi-polar Christianity, where one second we are trying to *earn* God's approval and blessings, and the next second we are *thanking* Him for them. Achieving in the law one minute, resting in grace the next. One second we say, "We built this," and we look down on those who were too "lazy" to succeed. The next second, with humility, we say, "Thank you, Jesus, for your blessings!"

THAT. IS. CRAZY! This is a terrible way to live. This is a terrible way to treat people. Bi-polar Christianity is not the abundant life; it is a terrible life.

What if we stopped living this way, and started living as if grace is the truth, the whole truth, and nothing but the truth? What if we actually functioned like every blessing flows simply from His grace? You never earned your degree; you received it by His grace. You never built that business; you were blessed with that business by His grace. You never kicked your addiction; you were given freedom by His grace.

This is consistent Christianity. This is humble Christianity. This is abundant living. This is a keg of blessings freely flowing to you and me all day every day because of Jesus' work on the cross.

What if you didn't have to behave
to make God happy with you?

What if you could live the good life without a list of rules?

What if God's favor was readily available to you?

It's paid for, and you can have as much as you want.

IT'S GRACE... ON TAP.

Now available on **Amazon** and **Amazon Kindle**.

How to be a Guide (a Sponsor)

Mission of a Sponsor: To walk side-by-side in life with another person as they discover the grace of God and the freedom that Jesus brings.

1. Relationship Boundaries

a. Ask if they are willing to follow your leadership and counsel.
   - If yes, give them an assignment to call you every day for one week, twice weekly thereafter. (If they can't call you when times are good, how will they call when it's bad?)
   - If no, tell them it's better if they find a different sponsor.

b. Give them a specific phone number to reach you, especially if it's an emergency!
   - They need to contact you. You are not codependent with them and are not responsible to hunt them down.

c. Let them know what you will or will not tolerate.

d. If your sponsee doesn't have a place to live, it is not your responsibility to find them a home. You are there to give guidance through the mile markers. Never, under any circumstance, let your sponsee live with you!

e. Your sponsee is not allowed to make unannounced visits to your home.

f. If you haven't heard from your sponsee in two weeks, call them to see how they are. Reiterate that they need to call you. If they are not able to stay in contact, gracefully encourage them to seek another sponsor.

g. They need to show up to the recovery meeting you attend.

2. Giving Direction

a. Walk your sponsee through the mile markers. You must know the mile markers well enough to have the ability to "do life" with your sponsee. Take them to lunch, read along with them, etc.

b. Squelch gossip about other attenders and leaders at your recovery meeting! It is your job to protect others in recovery. Gossip breeds fighting, and it is old behavior. If you practice this, give consideration to your readiness to be a sponsor.

c. Mile Markers 4 and 8 are inventory lists, and are simply pen and paper processes.

d. Mile Marker 5 meetings and Mile Marker 9 amend processes need direct coaching. Please know how to conduct this coaching before moving forward.

e. Mile Marker 12: Having been set free by the grace of God, we seek to bring freedom and grace to others as well. As a sponsor, this means that you're the messenger. You set the bar for where you'd like your sponsees to go. You are the one they see as grounded in faith. All of this means that sponsees don't make rules of how they plan to work their recovery program. If they knew how, they wouldn't need recovery.

3. Experiencing the Mile Markers with your Sponsee

a. All of the mile markers need to be completed and accounted for. This is your job as a sponsor.

b. Make sure they have completed and understand each mile marker before moving on to the next one.

c. Share your experiences of each mile marker and how it affected you.

d. Give assignments as needed. For example, give them deadlines to complete Mile Markers 4 and 8 lists, when you'd like to see them have reconciliation completed, etc.

e. Know what you don't know. If you don't know the answer as you sponsor someone, don't guess at it. This is a person's life you're dealing with. Take the time to get a hold of your sponsor or pastor to get good counsel and instruction as you guide your sponsee to the next level.

4. Help them Develop their Spirituality

a. Process through the Bible with your sponsee. Help them understand verses.

b. Share how Jesus and His grace changed your life.

c. Show them how your observe, study, and apply the Bible to your life.

d. Pray with and for your sponsee.

e. Make sure they are connected with the body of Christ by attending a weekly worship service.

5. Show them how to Help and Sponsor Others

a. Create apprentices for yourself so they can bring freedom and grace to others as well.

b. Teach your sponsee how to help someone in need.

c. Teach your sponsee the meaning of servanthood.

Discipleship Group Leader Guidelines

A discipleship group leader is different from a sponsor. A sponsor's job is to walk through the 12 Mile Markers with their sponsee. A sponsor's job is not building a leader. Sponsoring points people to hope, freedom, and health through Jesus.

Discipleship group leaders facilitate a group. Facilitating a group means ensuring the conversations in group are pointed toward solutions, not problems. Refer people who need help with their problems one-on-one to a sponsor. Remember to stress the importance of confidentiality.

Role of a Discipleship Group Leader:

1. **Love people and build relationships.** Help people understand how important they are and that you want to see them participate and come back to group to connect with others.

2. **Bring passion and energy to the group.** One of the major reasons people don't come back to a recovery meeting is because it's boring or it's focused on problems and triggers old behaviors. Your job as a discipleship group leader is to bring passion about Jesus and the 12 Mile Markers. Show them how exciting life in recovery is! Your job is to be so energetic about recovery that it pours out of you, so they see what might happen in their lives! Remember, people are looking for YOU at the meeting. If you want respect in your leadership, show people how passionate and energetic you are about your recovery meeting and Jesus!

3. **Service work.** If you want to see sponsees and participants grow, they need to own a job. Give them a specific, small volunteer job to be responsible for at meetings. When we don't put a value on helping others, we give an indication that we don't value people, and

they can sense that! The Bible says that Jesus came to serve, not to be served.

Running a Discipleship Group from Start to Finish:

1. Explain the discipleship group format (remind your group about confidentiality):

   - We pray.
   - We talk about the talk.
   - We talk about the mile marker we're experiencing with our sponsor.
   - We pray to close.
   - We stay around to connect and talk more (if needed), and please don't take offense if we signal you or ask you to wrap up the time you're sharing (we keep it 3-5 minutes each).

2. Pray.

3. Talk about the talk (have everyone share one point they learned from the message, reminding them to keep their sharing solution-based).

4. Talk about which mile marker you're experiencing with your sponsor.

5. Connect them to a sponsor if they don't have one.

6. Pray.

7. Clean up.

Launching and Leading a Recovery Meeting

Commitment Get a group of 10 people and dream big!
(Planning your launch takes 3 months)

    a. Every member commits to attend for one year.
    b. Every member commits to working the 12 Mile Markers personally and sponsors someone else.
    c. Every member commits to bring an addict friend to the launch.
    d. Every member commits to come one hour early and prepare, also to stay ½ hour late to clean up.

Groundwork

1. Find a space to meet. All you need is a room with electricity, bathrooms, and a space for kids.
2. Set a date for your launch.
3. Find a leader for each area of ministry:
   a. Worship leader who recruits a team/band
      Note: Ideally outside of the church worship team.
   b. Teacher
   c. Discipleship group leaders
   d. Kids Programming leader
   e. Set up and tear down leader
   f. Powerpoint and projector operator
   g. Sound tech
4. Partner with your Lead Pastor to sell the vision to the church.
   a. "Preach to the problem" for several weeks in advance
   b. Consider a teaching series about recovery/the 12 Mile Markers

Pre-Launch

1. Advertise. (We sent out a direct mail piece to our community. Ask your local newspaper to include your meeting in its community events directory.)
2. Hold two practice meetings to work out all the logistics.

3. Schedule, Appreciate, Apprentice, Inspect:
   a. Schedule training sessions with your teachers and leaders monthly.
   b. Appreciate leaders by investing your time and resources.
   c. Develop apprentices to grow up other leaders.
   d. Inspect to make sure the broken have red carpet treatment and there is unity in your leadership.

Launch and Beyond

- Plan your meeting strategically/have a standard operating procedure.
- Arrive one hour before the meeting and unlock entry ways/doors.
- Turn on heat/air conditioning for a comfortable environment.
- Put signs outside the building so the community knows you exist.
- Use signs inside to point out kids programming areas and small group meeting rooms.
- Put the chips/medallions on stage to hand out in the large group session.
- Get the offering containers ready; assign two leaders to collect the offering and a procedure for handling the money after it is collected.
- Have a "talk through" with the band, technicians, and teachers.
- Make sure the band or worship leader is rehearsed and ready to go.
- Make sure Powerpoint slides for the music and the message are ready.
- Clean all the floors and bathrooms prior to the meeting to make sure the space is inviting.
- Empty all trash cans and replace with a fresh liner.
- Set up food tables and be ready with food, coffee, and water.
- Turn on music so people have an environment that is exciting to walk into.
- Set up a resource table, including Mile Marker worksheets.

- Make sure all of the discipleship group leaders and kids staff are present and ready for the evening (we have a momentum meeting thirty minutes before large group).
- Pray and ask God for people to show up and for God to do miracles and change lives!
- Place leaders at the door to greet people as they arrive.

Meeting Schedule

5:30   Potluck Dinner (optional)

6:00-6:40   Large Group Meeting
- Worship leader or host welcomes the crowd and tells them our purpose (we are all about Jesus and the 12 Mile Markers)
- Worship music
- Prayer
- Host: Welcome, news updates, small teaching/testimonial segment
- Teaching piece (25 minutes maximum - focusing on teaching from the Bible and the Mile Markers)
- Host: Chips/medallions
- Give an offering together
- Close and release to discipleship groups

6:45-7:30   Discipleship Groups
            (refer to Discipleship Group Leader Guidelines)
- Break into groups by gender

7:30   Post-meeting Clean Up

Growing a Recovery Ministry

Growth factors for a successful meeting:

1. **Create a culture where people aren't judged.**
   Help your people understand that we're all jacked and fall short of God's standard. Nobody needs to sit in a corner in shame. Because of the grace of God, we have all been saved and we are not condemned, no matter our issues!

   ***Acts 15:11** We believe that we are all saved the same way, by the undeserved grace of the Lord Jesus.*

2. **Create a confidential, anonymous culture.**
   a. Help your people know how important it is not to share other people's personal issues with each other.
   b. Help your people be respectful of others, and never by any means bring up someone's confidentiality in public.

3. **Advertise! (This is not a secret meeting.)**
   a. Send out a postcard.
   b. Put street signs and directional signs around the church/meeting place.
   c. Put flyers out in your community.
   d. Empower your people to be the mouthpiece, hands, and feet of Jesus.

4. **Greet the hell out of people!**
   a. Help your leaders understand how awkward it is to walk into a recovery meeting for the first time.
   b. Meet people at the door and where they're at.
   c. Give people a personal connection with the teacher and pastor.
   d. Sit with the first-timer during group.

5. **TRAIN and delegate tasks to a leader.**
   a. Schedule, train, appreciate, inspect.

6. **Teach your people to own the house!**
   a. You don't want to be the only one doing all the work
   b. Give away leadership, not just tasks, and watch your people thrive!
   c. 3 things we teach our leaders: Love people, bring passion and energy, get people plugged into serving.

7. **Focus on the solution, not the problem.**
   a. Own the grace-based mile markers. Live, eat, breathe, and sleep the mile markers. You can't help someone else if you don't know what you're living out yourself.
   b. Give people a road map to success in recovery through sponsorship and small groups.
   c. The problem is what led to the addiction, the solution is Jesus and His grace while living in the flow of the 12 Mile Markers.

8. **Get people plugged in to church.**
   a. The greatest investment we can make into others is plugging them into a worship experience with Jesus.
   b. People need to feel needed and known. Help them to be connected to your church through volunteering or groups.

9. **Make sure every attender finds a sponsor.**
   a. Attenders of your recovery meeting have been doing life on their own and have come to your meeting for direction.
   b. Sponsors who have experienced the mile markers can help these people thrive and are the guide down the river of grace.

10. **Help broken people dream again.**
   a. Broken people haven't been able to dream for a long time. Help them see that Jesus has so much more for them.
   b. Create community events where broken people can come and build relationships with other people in the recovery experience. Thriving friendships are what every person wants.